BE GOOD
BE BRIEF
BE GONE

BUSINESS STRATEGIES FROM THE WAR ROOM

THE TRINITY OF SUCCESS

JASON MILLER
JAMES FOO TORRES
AND THE SAB TEAM

TABLE OF CONTENTS

FOREWORD

Picture for yourself a team of 10 assisting you throughout every aspect of your responsibilities, just for a day. Visualize someone optimizing your morning ritual to maximum productivity while another individual acquires the perfect cup of joe to your tastes. How much better would your day look? What kind of self-improvement could you engage in when you had the support of 10? Between 2016 to 2017, Jason Miller, Founder and CEO had this vision for small businesses and created the Strategic Advisor Board: a team of 10 serving as advisors to small businesses, helping them build customized solutions to strategize and grow. The team along with Jason shared their insights on small business secrets for success.

One of the magic ingredients to small business success is the team you surround yourself with. With 10 CEOs, SAB has a track record of small business success that speaks for itself. Will Black, VP and Director of Finance at SAB, shared how Hollywood often presents a glamorized version of small business that does not necessarily reflect the many challenges undergone and the hats a small business owner may wear when launching. As a small business is finding its footing, SAB provides 200+ years of lived business experience that a newly-opened or even mature company does not have access to.

A common struggle with small business owners, as Jason shared, is finding the right strategy to pivot when they have hit a dead-end in the market. Jason emphasized the importance of micro pivots within a small business environment. SAB is all about strategizing to fit small businesses' specific needs; whether it be launching for the first time, refreshing outdated systems, or rethinking an entire advertising campaign to progress a business forward. Mega-corporations have easy access to resources and financial leveraging opportunities where small businesses do not. Jason, specializing in strategy implementation, stated that SAB invests in micro pivots that are feasible and affordable for small businesses. Senior VP Shelby Jo Long spoke on the importance of financial strategy when facing challenges, saying "it's possible to weather the storm without expending too many of your resources."

Investing in the future of small businesses is an investment in the greater community, as Jason remarked that "small businesses are the backbone of America." According to SAB, over 80% of charity donations today are coming out of small businesses. A small business that is thriving in its market generates more revenue and invests more money back into its community. Part of Mike Jackson's specialty as director and VP of sales at SAB is looking at these revenue strategies to build a sustainable model for the future. Investing in charities from small businesses not only contributes to community thriving but also brings a larger sense of purpose and belonging to those involved. One of SAB's clients' first questions when they first met in person was "can you please tell us how we can help our charity?." Will Black remembers his sense of awe and honor to get to work in this field knowing these are the type of clients they meet every day. Joel Philips, director of technology sharing similar sentiments in that he is inspired daily by the people he gets to collaborate with.

You would be silly to buy a product that the designer did not use themselves; the same goes for small businesses and an advising team they trust. Some of SAB's own 10 were originally advised by Jason and other members of the team, so they personally testify in their own business success to the efficacy of SAB as a whole. SAB sets itself apart with the trust they build on a results-focused strategy. Clients don't pay a dime until they have seen results from SAB coming in to revolutionize their small business. SAB believes in a holistic model of advising that will empower the passion and drive of their clients to build a better business.

In the words of Mike Jackson, "every owner started their small business because they are passionate about the product they are providing." At SAB, Jason's team of 10 embodies the intrinsic crossover between passion for your business and a drive to succeed. Joel added there is "no one who is a bigger proponent of our product" than the team themselves, as they are all small business owners themselves and some have even been clients of SAB in the past. Small business exists because of the people who decided, for once in their lives, they want to work for themselves. SAB stands behind this and also aims to reinvest in the communities that have given so much to make America a place where small businesses can thrive.

Something the general public might not know is that SAB is composed of over 50% veterans. When the SAB team's book, "The Power of 10" hit the best-sellers list and "The Power of 10 Reloaded" hit International Bestseller, Jason had planned all along to donate 100% of the matched proceeds to the veteran community. They were honored with this opportunity that they accomplished in under 12 hours. Jason reiterated that he is amazed at the team he gets to work with every day, and the unique "superpowers" each of them bring to the table. When asked what makes it all worth it, Jason said it is getting to hop on a call with this team of 10 and a small business that may be struggling and find a strategic and effective way forward.

Forbes Magazine

INTRODUCTION

To truly understand the connection between the title of this book and business, it's important to understand the times we operate in as business owners today. Without a doubt, the marketplace continues to get noisier and noisier with service/product providers who all claim to be the best in their industry. Adopting this very short yet powerful philosophy will help you provide products and services faster and more often to those that you serve.

We need to **BE GOOD** at what we do and stand out from the crowd. Create a USP (unique selling proposition) that absolutely crushes your top three competitors in your niche. Produce results that make a difference for clients and do this in a way that projects a high level of ethical, moral, and legal standards. Simply put, **BE GOOD** at what you do and out-shine all your competition.

BE BRIEF in your interactions and provide the value to your clients quickly. Get in, deliver value, and get out. As a business owner, time is usually our worst enemy. Time is precious and every hour needs to be spent around profit-generating activities. Therefore, it is very important as you serve your clients to simply **BE BRIEF**, get your point across and provide your service clearly and concisely. We can't make more time in our day and the last thing we need is MORE FLUFF.

BE GONE, should be self-explanatory but it's often not. Once you have provided or fulfilled your goods or services, just **BE GONE**. Get out of the way and let the client do what they need to do to implement what you provided. Don't hang over them and try to sell them more "stuff." I have seen this fatal error take root in many companies over the years. It's one thing to continue to share value; that's not what I am talking about. Deliver the service and let your client execute. **BE GONE** until the next appropriate moment presents itself to provide the next product or service.

THE TRINITY OF SUCCESS

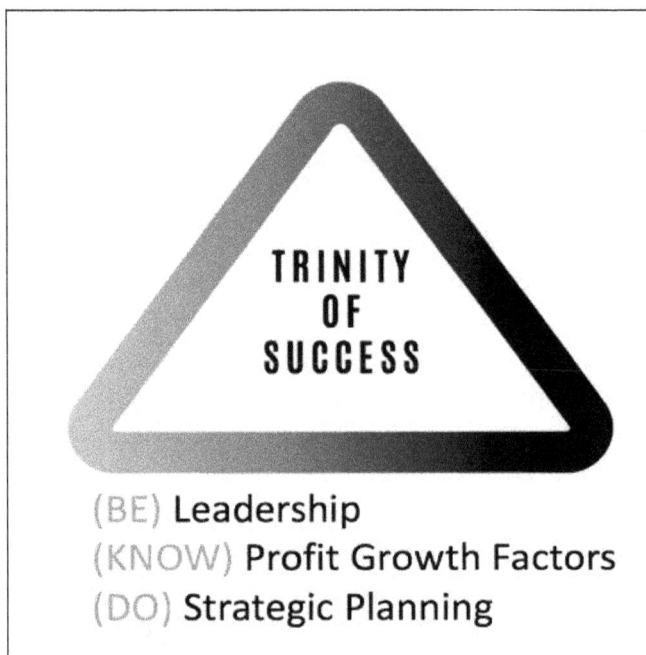

TRINITY OF SUCCESS

(BE) **Leadership**
(KNOW) **Profit Growth Factors**
(DO) **Strategic Planning**

This philosophy of **BE GOOD, BE BRIEF, BE GONE** directly coordinates with the system I created over 5 years ago. That system is called the **Trinity of Success** and focuses on three main areas to help you succeed in all your business endeavors.

Leg one of the Trinity is **(BE)**, we want to **BE** the best leader in our organization and lead from the front. Leg two is **(KNOW)**, we want to **KNOW** what our Profit Growth Factors are that will push us further and faster. The last leg of the Trinity is **(DO)** Strategic Planning. **DO** strategic planning that will allow you to push the limits of your company and backward plan from "exit" to where you are today.

In the world, we live in today, it is very important to adopt a system that keeps you on track. Keeping on track is more than just sales. We must create a system that supports our mission and vision while guiding the companies tactical and operational needs daily. Many companies simply lack a system or process that helps them drive the machine forward faster.

The last part of this introduction speaks to your continuity planning in life and business. Your life plan should be supported by your business plan. Take a hard look at the two and discover ways that you can balance one that effectively supports the other.

Over the last 20+ years, I have discovered pathways to creating cash flow for business. The system I have created increases revenue, but more importantly, increases passive income opportunity. Learning to work smarter, not harder, in business is the key to long-term sustainable growth that will support both your life plan and business plan in harmony.

Doing Good Is Good Business!
Enjoy the book and GO BE AWESOME!
Jason Miller

PART 1
WAR ROOM STRATEGIES

CHAPTER 1

QUICK WINS, SELF-DIRECTED LEADERSHIP, PROFIT GROWTH FACTORS, AND FOUNDATIONS FOR STRATEGIC PLANNING

The first thing that I'd like to introduce to you is the Trinity of Success. The Trinity of Success is a process that I created based off the amazing results I have experienced in my companies.

The Trinity of Success begins with self-directed leadership; that is something you must be: You want to be the self-guided leader of your company. The second part of the Trinity of Success is knowing profit-growth factors: You want to know the profit-growth factors within your company. So, the first step is to be a self-directed leader. Being a self-directed leader gives you clarity. Second is to know profit-growth. Knowing gives you focus. And the third part of the Trinity of Success is strategic planning, which you must do, and that gives you resource recovery.

To review, the Trinity of Success contains three important steps: be, know, and do.

Be the self-guided leader of your company.

Know profit-growth factors.

Do strategic planning for your company's future success.

All of us want to run successful companies. But what does that mean? What does that look like? What is a successful company? There are many definitions of success. Some people are happy with running a company that makes $100,000 a year. Great. It's not that hard to take that company, though, from $100,000 a year to $2 million or $3 million a year. It's not that hard; you simply must know and understand the factors to get you there. That's the simplicity of this training. I want to show you the way.

To grow your company, you must focus on three things: strategy, tactics, and operations. Those are the three things we're going to focus on in this training as well.

Let's start by clarifying roles and responsibilities regarding these areas of focus. A CEO must focus on strategic operations. Executives, executive administrators, and virtual assistants, focus on tactics. And the COO focuses on the operational side of the company. But these are three very different branches of the company. Now, does a CEO, president, or owner do the tactical things? Of course, they do; we all do. But it's about minimization of certain tactical things that many of you are doing right now that you should not be. Clarifying roles and responsibilities will help you focus on growing your company.

Most of you have heard people talk about working on your business versus working in your business. When starting and growing a business, most of us spend a lot of time working in the wrong way—not strategically. And the strategic plan is the most important thing. First quarter, that's the hustle. That is the time you set up the second, third, and fourth quarter for their biggest gains. In my company, the first quarter is my hardest time of the year. I work hard because come the third quarter, I take a month off and go on vacation. That's the way I like to do it. You work hard during the first quarter, and it sets the entire year up for success.

So, what is a tactical function? Tactical function, very simply put, could be something like handling the manufacturing of a product. It could be the fulfillment process. It could be training your staff. It could be the support functions in your business. It could be the administrative side of your business. Most business owners start the morning by checking their email. What is that? That's an administrative function. Stop it! Stop doing that, okay? That's not productive. The best time for you to check your email is before COB, or somewhere towards the end of the day. Stay away from it. Get off the social media and all that stuff. Your most productive moments are going to be in the first part of the day when you wake up, have that cup of coffee, and you're charged; you're ready to go. Your brain is functioning at its highest capacity at that point. So, don't waste your brainpower by checking your email. Instead, waste it with strategic planning. That's where you want to waste it. Strategy.

And that's not a waste of it because now we get into strategy; that's future planning, innovations, the who, what, where when, why. Your company's avatar creation. If you do not know what this is, you are cheating your company. You should know what they eat for breakfast, your avatar. Your client profile. And when you see the client profile that I've created for my company, you're going to go, "Holy cow! That is amazing!"

You'll look at that and be like "Wow! How can I create that myself?" I'll share it with you, that way you can just fill in the blanks, and that will help you identify who that is for you, who that is for your product, who that is for your company, your service, whatever it is your company does. This is vital.

To reiterate, you must be operating here in this strategic level. Period. And once you have this locked down, you will create success. Many of the clients that I work with, some Fortune Thousand, Fortune 500 companies that I work with, they can't get this right. They can't get that simple thing right. Who is my ideal client? You must know that, otherwise, what are you trying to sell? Don't go to a broad market; go to a narrow market that you can make tons and tons and tons of money from. Avatar creation is the first step in strategy, and one that you must not skip.

Next is operations. Operations is worst job in any company. Horrible. It is the most leaned on position in the company, your COO. That's the dirty job. The CEO gets to vomit everything to that COO to implement. That's the get it done implementation person. Some of you are that. You're the CEO, you're the COO, and you're the executive assistant. Some of you probably are doing all the roles. And make the investment to split this up and split away from it. If your company is doing well, if you're doing a couple hundred thousand dollars a year, at least, or even a hundred thousand dollars a year, invest in setting up your company correctly now because it'll be very painful to make those adjustments later.

So, operations, it's a key piece. They are the staff driver. I like to call them the company hammer. My COO is a direct reflection of me. It's like my hammer, right? A hammer is sometimes hard and sometimes soft. But they're going to drive your company from many, many different directions. Therefore, it's very important that these positions are segregated, and if you're doing them all yourself right now, if your company is in enough health right now, it's very easy to get away from this. These can be virtual positions, virtual assistants. Making these changes doesn't have to be expensive. It is fairly cheap to hire virtual assistants. A COO is another story. I'm a huge fan of the model called Rocket Fuel. And it's more the vision-ary/integrator. The COO would be both the visionary and the integrator. But it's a much different relationship from integration to visionary. Because a visionary truly sits from a 30,000-foot platform and has the visions for the company and then gives them to the integrator, the COO, to execute.

Next, let's discuss self-directed leadership. What is that? What does that even mean? What is self-directed leadership?

You are the guide. You run the ship. You're the north star for your company. You run that ship. There's nobody in charge of you. So self-directed leadership is huge from that standpoint. I spent a large part of my life in the military, and self-directed leadership is a big thing at certain levels. And you must get this right. If you're an owner-controlled company, you don't have a board pulling the strings behind you. If you're an owner-controlled company, there's nobody there to lead you. You must lead your company. That requires self-directed leadership. I'm not going to go on a rant and rave about leadership; however, it's key and important. Three things that you must remember regarding leadership are to be firm, fair, and consistent. If you do those three things from your seat, if you are firm, fair, and consistent with your staff, you will be an absolute success from your chair as the CEO, President, or whatever your role is. So be firm, fair, and consistent all the time.

Next, let's look at this from the perspective of a CEO. Everything you do needs to be from the perspective of a CEO, no matter what. Look at it that way, train your head that way now, that I'm the CEO of this company, I'm the CEO of my life, I'm the CEO of my destiny, so on and so forth. So, we need to really look at how we gain that focus through profit growth factors; how we know those profit growth factors. Now, this is not a completely new theory with inputs and outputs; however, it's how it's implemented that matters the most.

As a CEO, let's look at two completely different models. First, let's look at how we implement things. Our input is 95% strategic and 5% tactical. We can have a small, small, small input that's completely strategical that kicks out a very large output that creates more cash mid and long-term. And some short-term. But mostly mid and long-term. Remember, we work ourselves to death during the first quarter, right? Why? Input. Smaller input strategy create third and fourth quarter growth. We're not so much worried about today. If you're in a business and you need today money, then you have to think about that because today money is hard. That doesn't come quickly. If you do, you can flip this, but I don't ever suggest doing that because we want to plan for the long game. As of not too long ago it was 93% of small businesses that fail between year one and five. That's not my number, that's the Small Business Administration. So, we must be cognizant of this as a business and know how we strategically plan every piece and part of what we do. That's where this formula here, it may not create tons of today money, but it's going to create sustainable, long-term business, which is what we should all be looking for. Sometimes we must go through that little hard punch in the face in the beginning. We all did it. I did it. I shoestring budgeted my first two or three companies that I started. And the first company I started—and I'm not embarrassed to say it—I was selling Halloween stuff like flashing vampire teeth and flashing gloves and all kinds of weird stuff. From that, I learned a lot. I learned that strategy and outward planning are most important because if we don't strategize and plan for years, we're more likely to fail. Notice that I said years, I didn't say months, I said years. Plan for out years. That doesn't mean that plan doesn't shift, but it allows us to get away from doing these small little inputs, the tactical piece of this is bigger, and that's going to give us more on the backend, more on the long-term.

What is this going to give you? A lot of freaking work. That's what it is: It's a lot of tactical work. And you're going to have less here. You might get some quick cash, but if you're running a business for quick cash, you're not running a business; that's a hobby. You want sustainable growth. Sustainable quarterly growth over the next two-to-three years. Plan that out—for years. This leads to third and fourth quarter becoming a lack of dollar, a lack of money. Why? Because you have all this tactical input up front, all of these tactical things when you should have been focusing on the strategic. So, it's very important that for any business model, as the owner, CEO, President, whatever the case might be, you focus on strategic. Who is the best person that can sell a product in your company? Pretty easy question. You, right? You're the best person to do that. So, for example, I have referral agents in my company, and they go out and sell our services, and it's hard. It's hard for them to do that. Why? Because they're a representative of the company, where I can literally go downtown have a conversation over coffee, so on and so forth with somebody, and it's easy. Why? I own the company. I am the owner of the company. You are the owner of your company. You are the best salesperson for your company because you're the owner. That doesn't mean get locked into some operational sales process yourself, but

I'm just saying, be the cheerleader, right? Be the cheerleader for your company. Be connected within your community. Be connected within the Chamber of Commerce, maybe your rotary clubs, maybe your specific meet-up groups, give your time to go speak at meet-up groups, so on and so forth. Maybe nothing comes of that right away, but what is that? That is strategical punch, right? It doesn't come today. Mid. Quarter three. And long-term. Quarter four. These people become customers, clients, they like your services, they like your products, they pitch them for you. And now you're making money because you're the best cheerleader for your company.

I work with companies that are doing upwards of hundreds of millions of dollars a year, and they're not doing this. And these are owner-controlled companies, not board-controlled companies. Therefore, it's important that you know your role here. You must have this directional focus, and you know that this is your profit growth factor. You need to focus on this strategic piece. It's your job. It is your job.

If you Google "responsibilities of a CEO," there will be tons of places you can find basic responsibilities. They're all pretty much, for the most part, the same. That will give you a good guide of the responsibilities of what a CEO is supposed to do. Most of you are probably not following that. I have personal clients in my company that are breaching the Fortune One-Thousand list, and they're not following that.

What is CEO's number one responsibility? What in your mind do you think that is? It's very simple: P&L. P&L management. If you don't know what a P&L is, that's a profit and loss statement. That tells me that this month, I can spend this much. I know I have got X amount sucked up for operational costs, my final GP is this, I have this top-line revenue, and then at the end of it all, once it breaks out, I have a net income of Y. That is your north star report. If your P&L is not right, you need to get it right. If you don't have a good bookkeeper, you need to get a good bookkeeper. If you need a good bookkeeper, I have several that do very good work, and they can help you out. It's very important that your P&L is straight; it must be on target all the time.

So, around the fifteenth of every month when I get my P&L report, I look at it, and I almost immediately see ways that I could trim two percent off of it. Because do you know what a failure company looks like? A company that's paying $1,800 for a phone service. And I'm only saying that because I recently worked with a company, and I reviewed their P&L. They were paying $1,800 a month for a phone service. I pay about $200 a month for phone, internet, and TV for my company. There's no reason to be paying that kind of price for something like that. Now, maybe most of you aren't doing that, but there is often a lot to be shed off a P&L. And if you're not seeing it, you're not looking at it. It's like the quote see no evil, hear no evil, right? You can't operate a company that way. Therefore, you must pay very specific attention to your P&L.

So, we want to focus. All of you need to focus here on spending your time strategically in your company. Be the visionary. If you're doing all three roles right now, that could be for many reasons. Maybe you're just not at that life cycle yet. That's okay, for now. Just because a business has been around for three or four years, you could still be a start-up, and that's okay. The goal is to grow yourself, and your company, and do all the right things in between to make sure you get where you need to go.

All right, so let's talk about number three. How many hours do we have every week? You have the exact same 168 hours a week as I do. And I have grown companies from zero to hundreds of millions of dollars, pieced them out, sold them, and so on. You have the same 168 hours as I do. What are you doing with them? That's the key. What are you doing with them? Are you strategically placing those 168 hours every week to put them where they need to go? This is very important. So, what do we have here? We have productive timing. If you do productive timing, that means more money, right? Tactical timing, that's painful. Very painful. And tactics will cause your third and fourth quarter, I promise you, to be very painful.

Strategical time focuses on long-term, sustainable growth. That's what we all want, right? Heads up and down: yes. Long-term, sustainable growth. Say that over and over again. That's what you're shooting for.

There is a difference between growth and scale; these are two different things. People think they're the same; they're not. What is growth? Growth is people. It's employees. It's the things that drive the business. Scale is money. People and money are two very different things. I see variations of both done incorrectly. You may have a company that has outgrown its current scale model. What does that mean? I have 15 employees in my company, but my company only makes 10k a month. We've overgrown and under-scaled. This is a recipe for disaster. So, we want to do these simultaneously. And there's ways to do that so they're not so painful.

What you may need are TEs, or tactical executives. My tactical executives take all that tactical work off my plate. In other words, they do all the email filtering. I see what I need to see. When I open my email box, it's only the stuff I need to see.

My tactical executive has already taken care of the emails that are a waste of time for me. The TE has responded for me; they know how I think, know what to reply, and have taken this load off me already. So now, I can focus on strategical things, which is the scale, and I'm not paying a full staff because I might only need this person for one hour a day. And I don't need to pay them for anything else except that one hour that I need. But I know this person, they know me, they know what I want, I have the procedures and processes in place for us to work together successfully.

This leads to my next important point. I have these things in place now, so I don't have to explain it all the time. I have processes, roles, and procedures. These are vital and must be documented.

Let's say you have a great COO. They are doing a great job for you, but suddenly, they get a $100,000 pay raise offer somewhere else. And they're out. Money drives a lot of people, and you can't expect loyalty under these circumstances. So now what? What if that position isn't clearly documented? What if your COO role is unclear? If you're smart, you have that COO documenting the position the whole time they're working for you. They do it for you. If you're smart, you ask your employees from the beginning to document all of the things that they're doing while they're doing their jobs.. It is very simple. If you do have your employees document their roles, it is simple to bring a new COO in and say, "Here's your job. Here are the expectations, process, and procedure for your job." It's all laid out and clear, and everyone is on the same page.

By taking the steps that we've talked about so far, we have clarity. Hopefully, you're starting to see clearly what you are and what you are not currently doing. And then we focus on the profit growth factor. The know: know your growth factor. This is your growth factor from a COO's perspective. But you must know that growth factor for your company. What is going to produce the most bang third and fourth quarter? Second, third, and fourth quarters? Focus all your work, all your effort, all your strategical push, right now, during first quarter. Right now, this is the time to do it, so come August, you can tell your COO, "Here are the keys. I'm going to the Bahamas for the next thirty days, adios amigos." You might be thinking You're crazy. I can't do that. That's not possible. Of course, it's possible. It's absolutely possible. You simply must plan for it. If you plan for it and say hey, in August, I have a 30-day trip planned. Does this mean you get to unplug? No, that's not what I mean. You don't get to unplug permanently. That's not what I mean. I just mean this is your time, right? Maybe it's with your family, friend, or loved one. You recreate. You must recreate. That is recreating; you must do recreational things that recharge your brain, that relax you.

Every 30 to 60 days, I go down to Boulder, and I rent a room for two nights. I use that time to strategically focus completely away from family distractions. I will lock myself in a hotel room with Twinkies and Bon-Bons and Dr. Pepper for two days, and I come out all rashy-eyed and tired. But what I create there for my company, the strategical plans that I create for the subsequent either quarters or years or whatever the case may be, that's what drives my company. That's what the successful people are not doing. They're not doing that. They're doing hope. Ladies and gentlemen, business does not run off hope; it runs off of planning. Businesses are very mechanical. I'm not like the mindset guy and the universe guy and all that kind of stuff. But mindset does play a part in it. The right mindset, the right planning, the tools to do what you need to do to take things to the next level are all a part of building a successful business. And there's a difference between a company that's doing a million dollars and a company that's doing five million dollars. Up to a million dollars, you can do all of this yourself, pretty much. It sucks, but you can do it. It's doable. You start breaching that that, and this becomes very, very painful, to do all of this yourself. If you can, you're a very good manager of yourself.

However, we don't manage time. Anybody who says, "I have great time management," that's a joke. Nobody has time management. We have time allocation. So, we must make sure we allocate our time in the right places. We don't manage it; that's not possible. You don't get to control mother nature. But what you can do is allocate these 168 hours in the most effective way. And that is what's going to take you from that level of company you are today to where you want to be. This is where we gain clarity; focus here through profit growth, and then we must do the strategic planning. Strategic planning is resource recovery. Recover the resources because the next conversation we'll have is re-allocation. We recover, then we reallocate it in places it needs to go. Notice I didn't say we manage it. We don't manage anything, but we can reallocate it into these things right now, and this will free up a lot of your time. Goals, responsibilities, processes, procedures, so on and so forth. And it's all a very, very fine balance. Some of you have already learned this about balance. Balancing time, family, so on and so forth. What is a business there to support? You have a business plan, and but what's the purpose of your business? Your family, right? So, isn't that a life plan? Shouldn't you have a life plan? And isn't your business really designed to support that life plan? Isn't that why we're in business to begin with? Isn't that why we don't go to work every day downtown at whatever XYZ company as a service representative or whatever? We've built this dream, but why did we build it? To support this life plan. So, support that life plan. Make it happen. That's the whole point. Focus on your business so you can do those things with your family. That doesn't mean being a slave to your business. Nobody wants that. Nobody wants to be chained to their business to where they can't do the things that they want to do. Why? Because I am too busy every day. I work from morning until night every day. That's not fun. That's not a business. That's like dragging a chain around with you. Therefore, it's very important that you create the business plan that supports your life plan. Very important.

So, this is the part that's going to be painful. The part that will be very, very painful is called a time study. Nobody is going to babysit you on this; you either do it or you don't do it. That's up to you if you do it. But what we want to identify is what pieces are you doing tactically? What pieces are you doing strategically? What pieces are you doing operationally? And how do you do that? Here's how you do it: every 15 minutes, you document everything that you do. Every 15 minutes for the next seven days, for the next business week. If your business week is seven days, it's seven days. If your business week is five days, it's five days. It's a horrible process to go through. But I promise you, you will glean so much from doing a time study. It will show you all the tactical things you're doing that you shouldn't be doing. The knowledge you gain from a time study will be huge. And you'll probably hate me for telling you to do it now. But the point is later; come second quarter, you're going to be thankful about all the stuff that you off-loaded. It's amazing what I've got to offer. Just from doing this simple exercise. Nobody is going to force you to do it; it's up to you to do it. And then write those things that you're doing down every 15 minutes, and then after a week, go back and label them. Was that a tactical thing? Was that a strategical thing? Or was that an operational thing? Because that's directly going to drive this. How you spend your time determines your direction—and your outcome.

So, I challenge you to do a time study. Do it just to see where you currently sit in this lifecycle.

DEEP DIVE ON INPUTS/OUTPUTS AND LEVERAGED WORK

Another area of your business to address is inputs, outputs, and leveraged work. In this next section, we will focus on correct inputs, acquisition upfront; wrong inputs, the admin minutiae; working smarter, not harder; leveraged work. The outcome we want you to take from this is realizing that smaller actions provide bigger results if you do the right actions. Identify those time killers and increase profit. Cut out all the waste and move the needle farther faster.

First and foremost, we're going to talk about inputs, small actions, outputs, and big results. We want a small action to create a big result. And how do we do that? Well, let's talk about a small action on your input side. This is your big target. This is your focus. You want to put the least amount of actions, or things that you do to that front (input), to create a larger output. So, you want to get this right. Acquisition on the front end, for example, creates profit. That's an input, and it's a small action because that acquisition could be paid advertising, it could be your sales force, it could be many things, but those are actions that don't require you physically to do something. So that acquisition is a small action leveraged to create a big result. 98% of your time should be spent her,e and this creates higher profit margins. The whole point is to gain true growth and scalability.

When we look at the output side of things, this is to win. We kill waste, and we go all in. We want to define the goals that matter so we can really move that needle forward. You write these down and clarify how to get there, and anything that's not profit-generating goes away, period. And we really need to focus on that front part of this to define those profit-generating activities to really do the scale. Because at the end of the day, an input that's a small action that leads to an output with big results equals bigger profits, bigger margins, and scalability—that hockey stick scalability.

However, there is also the absolute opposite of that. There are large actions in the input that lead to small results for an output. These are non-revenue generating things. They include all the administrative minutiae. It could be checking emails. It could be messing around on Facebook. It could be getting caught up BS-ing with other CEOs on the phone. All things that are not profit-generating. I had one client of ours, they would spend at least two hours a day out shopping for the office, for groceries and office supplies. This is a perfect example of a terrible input. Two percent or less of your time should be spent on this kind of work. Errands are bulky, time-consuming, and not profit-oriented, and this is a do not do moment. Do not do this because this will impact your business in far more ways than you understand. Instead, we want to focus on small action input versus the large action input because you get a small output, small result; no profits or very little. It's not leveraged time; it often leads to bankruptcy, a big cash burn period, and a horrible ROI. This is really where you must focus on the things that matter in your business at your level. And that could be a lot of different things.

Our goal is to utilize focused work. We want to work smarter, not harder, and we want to do leveraged work. There is a model for this. It includes input, output, small input and big output, and big input and small output.

We have the resources that we put into the business, our input. And we have the resources we get out of the company because of the input, our output. Some resources or actions don't cost us a lot that we can put into the business, small input, that pay us huge output in return. These inputs could include smart advertising or a solid sales staff and sales process. All these inputs lead to money. For instance, lead generation funneled directly to sales staff is a small input for the company. However, it creates a large output, which means more cash in your pocket. More success in your business and cash in your pocket lead to scalability. Now, the point is to go all in on what really matters and cut all the waste parts because this will lead to growth and scalability.

Let's look at the other side of this. Let's look at the side of it of a large input and a small output. So now we have a very large input and a small output. When we aren't intentional about how we use our resources for our business, we often spend our time and energy on tasks that create a small amount of profit. When we're operating this way, it does not allow for scalability. This is where your company baselines out, and you're always doing a whole bunch of work up front but it's not the right work; it's not smart, leveraged work. This eventually leads to bankruptcy. And I always say this should be 98% and this should be 2%. All this stuff here is admin stuff. Admin, checking emails, you're on Facebook, you're doing all of these – I call them minutia actions because none of this stuff relates to cash.

My wife used to work for a four-star general, and there was hardly any of this stuff that he did himself. He had a staff that took care of all the administrative stuff so he didn't have to do large inputs there and he could focus on small inputs that would impact the greater military. This example isn't one that is cash producing, but it is a great example of smart business. The point is to get all the administrative stuff off your plate. Hire somebody to take care of that stuff and get it off your plate. Another example of this is a general contractor who was spending most of his time, his large input, running around in Home Depot and picking up wood, supplies, so on and so forth. He burned large amounts of time, and this large input upfront was only creating a small output, which meant fewer jobs. Why? Because he spent more time running errands when he should be out talking to people to grow the business. For him, that is the generating input. If he simply hired someone to run errands for supplies, he could focus more on his small input, talking to people and growing his business, which is the work that matters to create scalability.

Therefore, the first thing you must do is to define your goal that matters and move the needle. This is where you're going to move the needle. Write it down; write this stuff down. Create a map and clarify how you're going to get there. Are these your inputs that matter? What are those for you? And then everything else that doesn't generate money, all this administrative garbage, get it off your plate. Get it out of here. You don't need it. Get rid of it. And then define–really sit down and define every money-generating activity, and those should be the focuses here because that's what's going to create this hockey stick scalability.

To finish off this section, I want you to do a speed exercise. It only takes one minute. I don't want you to take a lot of time to process and think. Simply write down the first thing that comes to your mind. So go ahead and pull out a pen and a piece of paper right now, and I want you to rate your small actions that create massive results, the top three things. Go ahead and write those out. When you're done with that, write out your large actions that create no results, the top three things.

(BE) LEADERSHIP

Leadership is about action, not position or title. Be the leader. People respond to good leadership. Period. It is in all aspects of our lives, not just business. A mother is a leader in her home, a son may be a leader of a team sport, or the daughter the leader of the debate team. A group relies on the person in charge to lead them to success. A true leader is highly ethical, honest, and respected. Key in on what I just said. Ethical, honest, and respected. If your subordinates look at you from those viewpoints, they will absolutely mirror your leadership style.

In our society, we have leaders and followers. Are we all born leaders? Of course not. But we can hone our leadership skills;. The leaders I admire have all these things in common.

They think big, and they don't put a ceiling in place. Instead, no limits are set on how big or how much better something can be. They always think big.

Their goals are firmly set in place, and their eyes never comes off the ball. Firmly planted goals are very important.

They make sure that everyone involved knows the final product and goals. Here's an example. If you sell widgets, it takes X number of widgets to succeed, or you want to win that football game and ultimately the title. Know what you're going for. Have your eye on that ball.

Great leaders can get compliancy to orders very quickly and very easily. That is so important that your employees, your staff, even your sub-leadership are compliant to your orders. It's hard to get things done in your company if you don't have compliancy all the way around.

And finally, when goals are met, good leaders set new goals and raise the bar. So always set new goals once you meet an action target and set the bar higher. People will follow your lead willingly if you are honest, ethical, consistent and treat them with respect. Rewarding someone when a goal is met is always appreciated.

In addition to these, a good leader is often responsible for making hard decisions. Sometimes, they must offload someone who consistently hinders the group or team members who are not team players. However, through wisdom and making these hard calls, you can improve your self-respect and become an inspiration to others. How great is that? You win and so does your team.

(KNOW) PROFIT GROWTH FACTORS

Here are the five main profit growth factors.

Number One: Attract New Leads with Information Marketing

Today's customers are hungry for information. They want to educate themselves before they talk to a salesperson or make a purchase. Providing them with information up front can make your business more profitable because it helps you win the customers' attention, contact information, and ultimately, orders. It is helpful to post information on your website or social media accounts; however, if you want to acquire prospects and contact information, you should use lead magnets. These are free, informational-packed, downloadable special reports, white papers, or checklists that can be downloaded for free by filling out a form. The information doesn't have to be lengthy; it just has to be informative and promoted with an attention-getting headline. Promote the giveaway on your website and through social media, inquire the downloader, at a minimum, to provide an email address to gain the information. Be sure the giveaway includes a call to action to turn the lead into a paying customer. And don't forget to follow up on that lead.

Number Two: Use the Leads You Already Have to Get Paying Customers

No matter how you get your leads, if you're like many small businesses, you don't follow up on them as much as you should. In fact, chances are you only follow up on the leads you believe are hot leads and then you may only follow up once or twice. The problem with that approach is two-fold. First, you waste the marketing dollars you spent to get the lead. Second, it keeps you from having ongoing communications with prospects who could become customers. Those possible customers include individuals who are just starting to research their intended purchase and those who are ready to buy but who have other more pressing things demanding their attention when you call. If you ignore them, you're likely to lose the sale to a competitor.

Number Three: Add New, Related Services to Increase Profitability

Do your customers need and buy products or services that are related to what you sell now? If so, you may be able to spin out some new revenue streams by offering those new related items. Keep track of items or services your customers ask for and then do enough market research to find out how widespread the need is and whether you could profit by adding it. Don't skip the market research. You wouldn't want to stock up on an item and then find that only one or two people really want to buy it.

Number Four: Increase Order Size

The math on this is simple. If you have one hundred customers who each spend $50 within one month, you take in $5,000 dollars. If you get those same one hundred customers to spend $70 a month, you take in $7,000 for the month, which translates to more profit for you without increasing your marketing budget. To get order sizes to increase, learn and train your employees to upsell and cross-sell. If you're a physical therapist, for instance, you might encourage patients to buy stretch bands, ice packs, and other equipment from you so they can continue their exercise program at home. You might also be a reseller for nutritional supplements. Flyers in your waiting area and placing posters where patients will see them while doing therapy can all help sell additional services without your therapists having to sell. If you sell products through an online shopping cart, add a function that automatically suggests related products to the shopper.

Number Five: Seek Repeat Sales

You can increase sales and profitability without any major increase in your marketing budget by using email and/or text messaging to stay in touch with your existing customers. Even though they are satisfied with their purchases, if you don't stay in touch, they may forget about you and seek other sources when they want more of what you sell. Get those customers to stick with your business by sending them reminders to reorder and news about new products. If you sell seasonal merchandise, send them notes about new arrivals and special sales and discounts.

(DO) STRATEGIC PLANNING

Here are three strategic planning avenues.

Number One: Assess Industry, Competitor, and Customer Trends

The first step of any strategic planning starts with studying the overall market in which you are operating. How big is the industry? How quick is it growing? Who are the key competitors? How well-funded are they? What moves are they making? What are pricing trends? What products or services are your customers asking for? Are there any micro-economic trends at play? Are there any government regulation issues? You cannot set an effective plan for your business unless you truly understand what you are up against from an industry and competitive perspective. Think about this as an external evaluation of overall market trends that impact your business.

Number Two: Complete a SWOT Analysis on Your Business

A SWOT analysis critically evaluates your company's strengths, weaknesses, opportunities, and threats. It will show strengths in your staff, customer base, financial resources, sales channels, products, profitability, growth, etcetera. It will also show weakness in your staff, market position, margins, financial resources, competitive vulnerability, missing products, customer complaints, missing sales channels, etcetera. A SWOT analysis will also make clear the opportunities to enter complimentary markets, form alliances, raise funds, launch new products, pursue M&A activities, exploit customer weakness, etcetera. And finally, it will show threats around the economy, losing key staff, lack of financial resources, limited cash flow, falling prices, etcetera. Think about this as an internal evaluation of your business.

Number Three: Define Your Mission and Vision

Once the external and internal evaluation is done, you're in a good position to begin crafting your high-level mission statement and vision statement. Your mission statement speaks to why you exist. An example of a mission statement is: Our mission is to replace expensive offline market research with equal quality insights from social listening. Your vision statement speaks to what you offer and the direction you're headed. And all good vision statements should be quantifiable and time bound. An example of a vision statement is: We plan on driving $50 million in revenue from our industry-leading social listening platform within three years. The mission and visions statements are the north star statements that will guide all detailed decisions from there.

STRATEGIC PIVOTS

Let's talk about some pivots in the society we're currently living in today. Everybody knows that our economy is not what it used to be even a few months ago, even a month ago. Our economy is struggling. We have businesses closing doors left and right, right now. And how do we not only survive but also thrive? What are some ways that we can take the lead and pivot what we're currently doing in our companies to be more successful?

This is not all-inclusive, but I want to give you just a neat example of how a company was very creative and pivoted quickly. This company is a restaurant and bar in New York. In the epicenter of this current crisis we're in, they saw an opportunity. As a country, we were going through this massive toilet paper debacle of a toilet paper shortage. So, they started delivering or offering pick-up orders of five gallons of Margaritas and a roll of toilet paper. That's a pivot, ladies and gentlemen, and a very, very, very creative one. Super creative. Why? They saw a gap. Everyone is freaking out because we don't have toilet paper. Well, great, everybody loves booze, and they need toilet paper, so let's do an awesome promotion to combine both. You're hurting for toilet paper, you can't get any at the grocery store, well, we'll get your fix too. We'll give you five gallons of margarita during your sequestration and a roll of toilet paper to go with it. That is extremely creative. And that is an awesome pivot.

Here is an example of another pivot. This other company did a simple pivot. Instead of selling one kind of account that they had been selling for years, they switched over to selling a different type of account. This other type of account wasn't the company's preference, but they could sell it at a profit margin of 50 percent or greater. So, at that point, they basically had to face that they needed to directly manage the crisis. Despite loving one way of doing business, they had to choose the option that made up the difference.

Here's another good example. I work with several general contractors that do home builds, general construction, road construction, providing goods, and services like gravel, and I was able to envelop some of these companies because I service government contracts in several different spaces. Through this, I could get them connected into government contracts for goods and services as a sub under my company. I won't get into the details of that; it's a bit complicated. But that's a pivot, right? It's a pivot. We took that company from a month ago, when they were swinging hammers on a roof, to now they've rented trucks and they're delivering 800 yards of gravel to the Department of Justice somewhere or the Department of Defense. That's a pivot.

Think creatively in your company, what's a good pivot for you? It could be as simple as taking a product, pulling out a feature of that product itself, and making that a standalone product. It could be something as simple as that. That's a pivot. It's a small pivot, but it's a pivot.

Now, you could also take your big product and make it a product of a larger product suite. That's another way to look at it. The other way to look at it is a whole different avatar. Take a different set of customers and position your company into a new market or a completely new vertical. This requires you to use that six or seven-pound mushy thing that's wrapped inside of that casing in your head. With your product and your service, how do I pivot that? Focus on a different set of customers, maybe. What you might think your avatar is today may have changed. Like my wife, she's not going to go downtown and go grocery shopping. She only did that because we had to because Amazon was out of service where we live. But now, Amazon is back in service, we have our groceries delivered right to our door.

Most people used to shop downtown, but now many do all their shopping online. Right now is a perfect opportunity for every e-commerce company to thrive. Why? Everybody is home. Everybody. That's why my bandwidth sucks sometimes. Because everybody is home using Wi-Fi. And what are they doing? Right now, everybody is stuck at home right now. I work from home, so this hasn't greatly affected me. However, for many Americans, they are used to being out and about and are stuck home now more than ever. For most people, being stuck home isn't normal. So now mom's home, dad's home, the kids are home, and everybody is going crazy because they're stuck in close quarters. They can't go to the park or do the things they normally do. So, think about that. Think about that and think about how you can get your product right there in front of them. I already know the answer to that. You advertise; you put it in front of them. That's how you do it. Because there is tons of money flying across the internet right now. Tons of it. Huge amounts of money. Because everybody is home. And the economics haven't caught up yet to all of this. When that happens, you're going to see this tighten up in the next probably 30 days. But right now, that's still wide open. And this may impact some, but in certain price points or certain income bases, this has no effect right now. None, whatsoever. They're off spending money just like they would anywhere else. Capitalize on that. I don't mean that maliciously. I just mean, take your business, throw it in front of them, and sell, sell, sell, right now. This is a very important opportunity.

If you run a software-based system that you sell, look at ways you can change a platform. Some are from a certain software to an app, but there's another way, which is an app to a software. I have clients that are doing that; they're flopping those back and forth. It could be an entirely different revenue model. For example, I guess probably the best in e-commerce would be an ad-based revenue model. Scale that. Scale ads. Many of you don't have stores, and if you do, the doors closed during COVID-19. But that allowed you to have this great opportunity to continue to scale your company through marketing that service or product. Through ad spend. Any good marketer will tell you: paid traffic wins. All day long. Any good marketer will tell you. There is no such thing as free traffic. It doesn't exist. And I can tell you right now, I have tried all of it over the last ten years. I have tried it all. I have tried going to fiber, doing the $125 SEO package for eight million gazillion hits in a month. Nothing. It's just junk. It's junk traffic. Put your money into places that are more certain when it comes to advertising. But that is your revenue model right now. That's my revenue model right now. We're eating our own dog food on that. I'm not just telling you that ad spend is the key; I'm doing it too right now. Why? Because I've seen a gap in the marketplace to do it and hit the audience that my competitors are not getting, and I'm going to capitalize on that.

Some of you may get manufactured products from overseas. How can you get that same product here in the U.S. from wholesale? How can you cut down on shipping times? There again, going back to fulfillment: if you can't fulfil, you lose. Most of you scale your ads to produce all the sales that you wanted to do given the right ad budget, condition, etc.; however, if you can't fulfil it because your fulfilment house is in China and you can't get that product over here, now you're in trouble. So, start looking for more suitable places for your product and service here. And you might pay more, but that's okay. Just pass that price off to your customer. People get so caught up in getting products from China. Who cares? It doesn't matter. Pass that price off to your client, your customer. If you're not pricing yourself far out of the market, it doesn't matter. Why? Because people buy value. And you're creating that value. It's a premium service. If I put a premium service together, it can be the same as the next guy, but people automatically think that if it's premium, it's got to be better! They think that it must be better. People will look at the same piece of steak cooked on the grill the same way, but if one is more expensive and has a brand name, they will assume it is superior. People put a luxury type fee on brand, the ambience of the restaurant, all these different things. McDonald's isn't going to sell a steak for $30. It's not their model. But a steakhouse is going to sell their steak for $30. So, make yourself premium.

I had this conversation with somebody not too longer ago about purses and a clothing line. They get it from China; it's a wholesale product, and anybody can get them. But people will be brand loyal if they think the product that they are buying is a premium product. Let's face it, 99% of the product in the world comes from the same place. There's eight different conveyor lines in a factory, they're all just getting a different brand put on them. It's called private label; that's all it is. This includes supplements, all of it. It's all the same thing, just in a different jar. I can't imagine I blew anybody's mind by saying that, but most products are that way. I could decide today that I'm going to go sell Vitamin C with a kick of Taurine and call it the best Vitamin C in the world. I could drop $5,000 into it, and it could be on the production line and shipped out to our distributors in less than a week, and the brand is born. It's not hard to do at all. Not at all. Now, don't go try to chase that down, please. Stick with what you're doing. I'm just saying, we create luxury within our brand. And focus on that, creating luxury.

Reliability is also a factor. A lot of times with products from overseas, the quality isn't there. And I know that for a fact because in the first business I started, back in 2000, I sold everything you could possibly imagine, flashy vampire teeth to soap and jock straps, you name it, and it was all from China. Everything was from China. And the upstairs of my house looked like a warehouse. I had a hundred flashy teeth here, flashy gloves there, all pre-boxed. And I'll tell you that the return on that stuff was 150 percent to 200 percent mark-up, but a lot of the time, the quality suffered. I could have gone with a U.S.-based distributor and gotten it wholesale for a little bit more and had a better-quality product.

So, think about pivoting your company now to position it in its best way. If you're getting sales right now, and a lot has changed, it's time for you to take your foot off the brake and press down on the gas pedal. Now is the time. It's a simple formula. Everybody is home. People are bored, they're online, and they're shopping. Why? Because they have nothing better to do. I can only speak for my household, but I can't even imagine how much online sales have been increasing. Why? Mama is on the computer all day. Add to cart. Add to cart. Add to cart. All day. Normally, most people don't sit home on their computers all day. But now, most of us are stuck home. Therefore, online sales are up. Capitalize on that. But capitalize on that for the good, obviously, because doing good is good business, right? Do good, and you can't go wrong.

CHAPTER 2

PROFIT MAXIMIZATION AND HYPER-GROWTH, DELEGATED TACTICAL TASKS, AND PROFIT MAXIMIZATION

In this section, we will continue working with the Trinity of Success. Remember that the Trinity of Success contains three main parts: the be, the know, and the do. In the last section, we talked about finding the resources. Now, we will talk about how to reallocate the resources. Resources could include time, money, staff, etc. When we talk about delegating tactical tasks or tasks period, these could include tasks that you simply don't want to do. Eventually, you will get to the point in your business when you start to pinpoint these tasks. You may start to think, I spend a lot of time doing this task, but I don't want to do it anymore. I have tasks that are probably CEO-level tasks, but I have an operations manager that I've hired to take them over. In one business that I have, I have a GM that runs the whole business; I'm essentially hands-off. Despite handing off tasks, it is still important for you to keep your finger on the pulse with everything, but you can still make decisions about how to reallocate certain things inside of your business.

This all leads us back to the importance of having an aligned focus for all those tasks that you're currently in charge of. In the last section, we talked about the importance of your time study. You'll never have that level of clarity about how you spend your time if you don't do it. Remember, you must write down every 15 minutes what you're doing and capture that for a week. Capture it for five days. People often hate me for telling them to do this, but a time study will allow you to figure out your priorities and where to allocate your resources. Fortune 500 CEOs do time studies every quarter. So don't think that you're exempt from doing them just because you're a small business; that's just an excuse not to do it. It's painful. But I do it every single quarter to find out where I can shave things off my business, whether it's time, cash flow, or P&L management. It is so very important that you do this.

I'm not here to hold you accountable to do a time study. Ultimately, it's up to you to do it. But if you do it, you can find out the problematic areas that you should be outsourcing. Your time study is central to aligning the focus of your business and your resources. I know it's a bit painful to do it for a whole week, but if you stick with it and do it for every 15 minutes while you're sitting at your desk working, you'll have clarity about the time that you're wasting.

And clarity is how you're going to get focus in your business. How can you focus in your business if you don't even know where your time is being allocated? If you don't know where it's allocated now, how can you reallocate it later? This is the foundation. If you have a good foundation built where you're handling the things that are more in a visionary role and then you have all those other tasks that are just ankle biter tasks that are happening throughout the day that you have outsourced and reallocated to virtual assistants or other staff. I mean, everybody here is at a different life cycle, so if you're currently in an office space and you have two or three employees, look at that workload and make sure that you're not working more than the rest of your team is working. And I see that stuff all the time. So that aligned focus is very important.

And this all starts to come now to the synchronization of your business plan and your life plan. What is a business designed to do in the first place? Business is designed to support what? Your life plans. That's what you want. Ideally, you want to be able to forecast the outcomes of your business quarterly. For me, I know what my business is producing so I know come August, I can uproot my entire family and we can go on a month-long vacation somewhere. Are you truly ever turned off? No, not really. You can't just turn it off completely as a business owner, but your business plan supports your lifestyle. I hate to use the word employee, but you are an employee of your business. I mean, that's what we are, we're just self-employed. But we run a business to live a certain lifestyle.

When you work downtown at someone else's company, it's the same thing, only it's a predictable lifestyle; it's not going to change most likely. You might get a raise this year, but it's not going to be that much. Whereas here, raises are going to be incrementally huge because you can go from a $100,000 business, a six-figure business, to a million-dollar business in one year. That's a lot different than working downtown. And now that supports your life plan. Or I like to call it the bucket list. I have a bucket list of things that I like to check off, things that I want to do in my life, and my business supports that because it costs money to do all that stuff. So, syncing all these things together is a direct reflection of delegating the right tasks to free up time for you to be the visionary of your company. But in order to sync these two things up, you have to do a time study to identify what those things are.

And reallocation isn't only for tactical tasks. It's for delegating tasks period. Because as business owners, what do we like to do? Hold it. Hold it. Hold it. Right? So, we often think, I'm the only one that can do this. No, you're not. Somebody else could do that. This is where documentation is so important. Documentation supports aligned focus. Now you have somebody doing a job, they're focused on that job, they know exactly what they need to do, it's documented, and if, for whatever reason, they leave your company, it's documented. You hire someone else, give them the Google doc of their job description, and they're off to work. And I see companies all the time making the mistake of not doing this. They'll have a COO that they hired 15 years ago. The position itself is not documented at all. He gets a better job somewhere else, boom, he's out, and the job is not documented. They hire someone else, but there's no processes, procedures, none of that documented. So, we want to make sure that all that's documented. That's focusing your business.

And again, I'm not going to ask you guys to send me your time study and review it and do all that kind of stuff. I don't do that. I'm a strategist, and I don't hold people accountable; I just tell them what can fix these problems. You must make these fixes. Some of this depends on what point in the lifecycle you are right now. Let's say you're making $50,000 or $60,000 a year small business; you can pretty much do all the work. A lot of businesses are doing most of the work themselves up to a million dollars. That's tough, but I know business owners who do it. But you better be willing to leverage all those hours per week. You're going to work, work, work, work, work. And the simple fact is you could be paying four or five people $8 an hour to take a lot of that load off you throughout the month, so why wouldn't you want to do that?

Anyway, so do this. Take the time to do the time study. You'll learn a lot about yourself in that process. And learning about yourself, it'll change some of your habits because we all have them; we all have habits.

Now, let's talk about profit maximization. You must be able to look at all your product line, all of your service line, whatever your business is, and maximize in every single area you can. Again, this is something that a lot of businesses don't do right. They don't even know what their margins are. There are no sharp profit increases. They don't exist because they're very linear across one product. There are no up sales, down sales, cross sales, none of that stuff, and that's really, important when we talk about product mix and up sales, down sales, and cross sales. Let's use purses as an example. I'm not a big fan of devaluing your brand by offering coupon codes. I'm not a huge fan of that. But it's all about a process, right? It's about a cart process. So, in other words, somebody is interested in a handbag, and they go through the current process to purchase, from there, what is the bump? It's called a bump. What's the bump up? Is there something that can be added that's cheap? Maybe it's a fragrance or a lotion or something. For an extra $4.99, we'll include that in the package. It's called a bump or an upsell. You might get 30 percent of people who opt in. Maybe it's only 30 percent at $4.99, but times a thousand customers it becomes significant. Additionally, the bump could even be why people purchase this handbag. The bump might be the wallet that goes inside the handbag for a 10 percent discount for purchasing today, but it's not really a discount. When you go to most of the stores to go shopping, and they're having a sale, it's not really a discount because they've already figured all of that into their product pricing. So, when you figure product pricing, you should figure that in there. Assume you're going to account for approximately 10 percent rebate at some point and then sell them as normal. This is standard across big box stores as well. You're not really getting a discount; they already figured that in the base price because they knew they were going to run discounts.

Now, when we talk about margins, you need to know your margins. Margins are vital. I'll use this one specific example. I worked with a plumbing company two years ago. They brought me in to look at their business and strip it apart from a mechanical standpoint, from product sales, profit margins, everything. So, we used one simple example, and that's water heater installations. They've been doing water heater installations for about ten years. By the time we stripped down that product, and we stripped all the expenses off that, he was going in the hole $200 per installation, and he'd been going in the hole $200 per installation on that for years. So, know your numbers. Make sure you've got decent margins. Your net margins should be at least 30 percent. What's the point of running a business if it's not paying you?

I worked with a recruiting company this year and their net profit margins were 8 percent. Why even own a business? That doesn't even make sense. You might as well just go to work, be an employee, and not work 100 hours a week. So, it's very, very important that you know these numbers. They're not hard to figure out; you just have to do the math. And that's taking all your operational costs that you have in your business and then start stripping all of that out in your products. Operational costs include VAs, office space rental, and all your expenses, which should be reflected in your product price. We all know that it's not rocket science. The problem is that people don't do it. They swag it. Don't swag stuff in your business. Know the numbers. Know the numbers and get it right.

Upsells work best when you're selling a physical product. Physical products create the greatest opportunity because people simply choose yes or no in the moment. If they don't want it, they just say no thanks. But statistically, 30 percent of people, as long as it—don't quote me on this, but say this product is $49.99 and it's a handbag or something. Most people will correlate these two numbers together and as long as this number is a small number, like the magic number $7.99 – that's one of the magic numbers is $7.99, especially in the physical product piece, because that's just a value-add, throw in the box. It doesn't really change your shipping, it doesn't change any of that, and it's cheap enough where they're curious enough, probably, to buy it, or at least a percentage.

There's a digital education company and most of the educational products that they sell are less than $8. This is close to a billion-dollar company, and they have massive amounts of courses that they sell, but they sell them at a reasonable price. They don't sell them at these price points of $6,000, $7,000. People aren't paying that for information anymore. People want value-driven education to move them forward. So, this digital education company sells their affordable courses and then they'll add an upsell for a cheaper price, a matching cart item. They're basically saying, "Oh, so you want to take this training, we also recommended these trainings too," and maybe there's five or six different trainings, and they're offering a deal for all of them for $30, so it's only $4 a pop. This is how you maximize your profit—by adding these little bumps.

Some of this is just split testing and finding that sweet spot. Again, the goal is to find the sweet spot. And I'll give you an example of an initiative that I'm working on right now. I've brought 15 different agencies together on this big initiative, and it's a white-glove service all the way through. So instead of an agency fighting the weed monster all the time for their services, now, it's delivering contracts. Here's how it works. A lead house produces leads to an outside sales team and then that outside sales team fulfills an actual contracted client to an agency. These are premium level agencies that are selling products for $10,000 or more, not small products. But they hand them over to a handler, and that handler then gives them white-glove service throughout the fulfilment process. So, the beauty behind having a high-end, meticulous service is that's how you get people to come back repeatedly. And don't think just because you're selling a product that you can't be meticulous and white glove because the simple fact is most people aren't high touch in the product business, and they're leaving a lot of money on the table because of it. They're not building relationships with their customers. It's hard to get the customer. Therefore, it is worth building a relationship with your customers and offering an incredible level of service, so they become repeat customers. Additionally, getting new customers costs money. So it is better to build repeat customers than putting all your time and energy into having to constantly get new ones.

It doesn't cost money once they've bought because now, we can market to them, we can give them white glove service, we can build that relationship with them depending on what your business model is, and they'll keep coming back to you. And at that point, they're not as concerned with the prices of your products. People still have brand loyalty these days if you treat it right. Does Walmart have a brand loyalty? That's debatable. But a lot of little companies have massive amounts of brand loyalty, and it is vital for your company because it allows you to find your sweet spots. And finding you sweet spots will help you find ways to increase margins. Your price points may not even be what you think they should be. Why settle for a 30 percent profit margin when you can get 50 percent? In some cases, in the product world, people are paying $2 or $3 for a product and then selling it for $50 or $60; that's a great profit margin. Still, do your math, strip it all out, and find your sweet spots.

Regardless of where you're at, you must know your company's numbers. At any point in time, someone should be able to ask you: What are the net profit margins in your business? What are your numbers? Do you have a P&L? What are your operational costs, and how are they split? Can you see how it chisels down to your net profit? This is all important information. And if you don't have a software to support that, I really suggest you do that because you can get a lot of data from software, and it will make it simple to have this information on hand and available.

Okay, so find the sweet spot. Manufacturing, direct, and wholesale are all great avenues. And again, I had a client that was paying $1.25 for a product straight from the manufacturer. And he'd been getting it straight from the manufacturer for probably a year or so, and we went back to the table and renegotiated that whole thing and he ended up getting them for 99 cents. So, make sure, if you're working with a factory direct deal, get the best deal that you can get. It can be challenging to get reduced prices if you're just doing stuff through a wholesaler. Sometimes they'll come off the price a little bit, but not usually.

All right, so now we move into hyper growth. How do we hyper grow a business? Well, it's simple. We start putting these pieces altogether. And then we focus on resource allocation. And if you learn to do this correctly and implement these strategies, you will recover and reallocate a lot of time and possibly a significant amount of money that you're allocating to the wrong places. It's important that you're investing in yourself and your business and most importantly, separating a hobby from a true business. Those are two very different things. You must put the capital, the time, and the effort into a hobby if you want to make it a business. Apple started as a hobby, Microsoft started as a hobby. Many businesses started as hobbies, and then they turned into true businesses. You're the only one who can differentiate that.

And when you invest in your business, the point is to hyper grow that business and reallocate these pieces that you identified as things that were either money savings, product market testing, and so on and so forth. I assume some of you do that with physical products; you test the marketplace. And then make sure that your product or your service is the right thing for the market. You understand that just because you love a product, it doesn't mean other people will love that product. Test the market first. Do pre-launches, do pre-sales first, and then launch into the marketplace, and that's what a lot of people do not do. They simply assume that because they love a product, everyone else will as well. If you bring a new product line in, test it first before you get crazy and start warehousing a lot of product. The same goes for if you offer a service. It all starts with knowing your customer. Build that customer avatar. Know your avatar. Know who your audience is. If you know that, you're drastically going to increase your sales. The more in-depth you get with that, the better off you're going to be. I always say you should know your ideal customer down to what they eat for breakfast.

Hyper-growth is hockey stick growth. It starts out slow and gradual and then takes off. And we can do that kind of growth if we infuse the business with what's required. What's required? You grow through people, process, procedure. How do you scale? Scale is through monetary. But they must be done together; you have to do them simultaneously. Otherwise, you get yourself in a situation where you've grown past your monthly budget or what you're bringing in. Then you're paying employees more than what you're bringing in. And I see that a lot in small companies because they don't want to let people go, so they struggle for months and months and months, and then they become the 93% of business failure.

So put all that stuff into place and again, it all comes back to your time study. How do you know where to focus if you don't even know where your time is going? If your time is spent on chasing around emails from customers, don't do that stuff. You can hire someone for that, and it's inexpensive.

Do the time study and figure out where your time is going so you can then reallocate it to the place that makes the most sense. We all burn senseless time; nobody is ever going to say that we don't, throughout our week, have time that couldn't be allocated in different directions; we all do. But we can maximize that with the most potential possible and put that time into investing in the business and investing in yourself. It's like I always tell people in my industry. I only work with executive-level, C-level type business owners and there's always time, no matter what. There's time, even with a big, huge company, that they could be investing more into their business from a 30,000-foot platform versus being so in the weeds. Because when you truly get to start looking from a 30,000-foot platform at your business, which is what I get to do with most businesses, it's easy to see where all the leaks are in the bucket.

And knowing where the leaks are is important because business is what? It's very mechanical. You do A, B, C to get D as a result. It's not rocket science; it's not rocket science at all. But it's making sure you've done the things, not just for your business, but for this plan: your business plan and life plan.

DEEP DIVE ON THE SALES PIPELINE (GROWTH-SCALE)

Next, let's talk about the sales pipeline, growth and scale. Areas of focus include the principle six, growth and scale solutions, and direct pipelines versus overcomplicated pipelines. And the outcome for today's lesson is properly mapping the process, that's huge. In order to do that, we must find the blind spot ID and get to the cause—the why, how, and what, and fix it.

There are six principle things in the sales pipeline. They include:

- Acquisition
- Lead nurture
- Conversion
- Value
- Fulfillment
- Deeper produce conversion
- Repeat

The first step is acquisition. Without acquisition, obviously you have no profit, no lead generation, no way to continue the process, so your acquisition plan must be wired tight and good to go. Once we acquire a lead, now we must nurture that lead through a process. That process is designed to nurture that lead through to the next step, which is the conversion. The conversion is the sale. Then, most importantly, and usually a huge bottleneck in the pipeline, is value delivery or fulfillment. Fulfillment is huge. Many companies struggle with the fulfillment end of it, and it's usually one of the largest bottlenecks. And this is where I usually tell companies to go through your own process in the background, go buy a product, watch how you're nurturing through either auto respond or messaging, sales teams, so on and so forth. Go through that process silently as the CEO to identify your bottlenecks. A lot of time is spent in fulfillment. From there, conversion, and now we work upsells and/or down sells. And then it's the rinse, wash, and repeat. Those are the six key components of the process.

So now we go to growth/scale solutions. We want to map this process from A to Z. We'll start with initial lead generation all the way through however you're selling your widget. Whether that is through phone calls, email follow-up, or a call center, it is important to have that entire process mapped. And then identify through that entire process what are the major blind spots in your process that you need to fix quickly and then get to the cause of those bottlenecks: what is the cause? Maybe the cause is your sales process. Maybe it is a specific delivery piece. It could be a tech piece. There is a lot of things that could create bottlenecks. And then identify the catalyst. The catalyst is the who, what, when, where, and why. Who is that? What is the catalyst to that bottleneck? Like I said, it could be something just as simple as scripting for a call center. If the sales scripts are off, that will negatively affect your business.

It could be many, many things depending on what the actual widget is. And then make the appropriate shift. And appropriate shifts are what's going to increase your productivity all the way around, but we have to be able to make those shifts in the pipeline to be able to productize and profit on our products in the best way possible.

Next, let's talk a little bit about over-complicated pipelines versus super direct pipelines. Over-complicated pipelines are very time-consuming to build. They're time-consuming to build, they're often very clunky, the salespeople or process that goes into them usually has a very difficult time maneuvering the process, and they create additional stress for a sales staff to figure out that elusive process sometimes. Operability, it's a higher cost to maintain, especially for new hires, because training must be so deep. And then most of the time, complicated pipelines end up being replaced anyway. So, let's really focus this whole thing on clean line, direct pipelines, because typically, there's not as many bottlenecks; the bottlenecks in the pipeline will only be within the principle six steps. You'll have less bottlenecks because you'll have less working parts, less process to really stress on that sales staff, and it will be far easier to maintain and tweak from a tech standpoint. Plus, you'll always get higher ROI and faster and more profitability when you're selling your products or services or whatever that is to your customer, and it's, generally speaking, easier to deliver that service or product if we stay in a very direct pipeline where each of the principle six steps is easily executed without too many offshoots into other things or other places where we're taking the customer through different journeys. Therefore, we want to be very careful about how we set up our pipelines; the more direct pipeline for a widget we have, the better off we are. That doesn't mean it's remiss of upsells, down sells, things of that nature; it just means how we structure it is very to the point and gives the customer a simple journey through the sales process.

Now that I have introduced you to the principle six, let's talk about how to put those into a simple pipline. Remember, the principle six include: acquisition, lead nurture, conversion, value, fulfillment, deeper product conversion, and wash, rinse, and repeat.

We always start with acquisition. Once we gain leads through acquisition, we begin nurturing our leads, whether that is through a sales process, a layered stack of phone calls, whatever that might be, and this depends on what kind of acquisition we are doing. If this is a lead acquisition, it's going to differ from paying client acquisition. However, either way, we want to nurture through that process. Then, we come through to the conversion. Now, a conversion means a lot of things. A conversion doesn't just mean a sale; a conversion can mean they got a free product of yours. They were still converted to something in your business. So don't always look at conversion as it's only a sale because it could be other things. Once we get that conversion, the actual sale here, depending on where this process is, we get the sale that happens, now we have to deliver and fulfill that product. This is usually a major bottleneck. The largest bottleneck is normally in delivery and fulfilment, and if you don't have this right, this is where you start to lose a lot of business and a lot of continuity. A lot of this falls on your support staff to make sure they're doing good follow-up with your customers and then taking that input from your customers and creating the best service and product possible. Once you nail down the delivery and fulfillment, you can install a deeper conversion, which is an upsell of another product into a down sell.

And from there, we get to the money part. Where most companies don't do it right is they don't continue to do the follow-up to continue monetization. This is huge. Continue to monetize this customer through another avenue. Maybe it's a continuity program, we'll talk about that soon.

Where it starts to get complicated is when you start putting too many layered pieces into this. If you add too many additional steps, instead of following the principle six, you start to lose a lot of people through the process. It is best not to overcomplicate this. Stick with the principle six. Will you still lose people through the process? Of course, you will, but not as many as if you overcomplicate the process.

Okay, let's hop on into this speed exercise. You have one minute to do this speed exercise. So first, what I want you to do is to identify: What are three sales pipeline successes where you have it right? And then, what are three sales pipeline failures where you have it wrong? Look at your sales process and think about what parts are going well. Also think about what parts aren't going well. Don't process through this too deeply. Write down the first things that come to mind off the top of your head: the top three things you know are having issues with and the top three things that you know are successes.

(BE) LEADERSHIP

To grow, scale, and win, you must be a leader. Great leadership is the key to success. Let's discuss some absolute key characteristics of a great leader.

Great leaders are great communicators. Great communication is the key to great leadership. Think of any greater leader in modern time: Gandhi, Martin Luther King Jr. and John F. Kennedy. They were powerful leaders because they could inspire people to follow them. It was their ability to articulate their vision that made them successful in achieving their goals.

Great leaders inspire others. In your organization, you must be the leader who inspires the team to great heights. To get them to follow you, be sure they are listening to your values and your vision, and then establish the right environment for them to thrive and grow.

Great leaders are value driven. Solid values drive your business. When I mention values, everyone nods their heads as if, of course, that's obvious, but when I check up on this piece, I find the last time that they discussed their values, personal and professional, with their team, was often in the interview before their people were even hired. You must clearly know your personal values and your organizational values to lead effectively. For example, do the answers to these questions come readily to mind? Personally, what do you stand for? What is most important to you? What would you like your life to demonstrate? What is your personal mission in life? Now, professionally. What do you stand for? What are you willing to do to get new business? What are you not willing to do to get new business? Do you have a professional mission statement? Quality leaders don't change their values over time or to achieve short-term success. Consistent, core organizational value systems form the strong foundation for long-term success. A simple definition is that your values are the rules by which you play the game. A well-defined value system makes all decisions easier and encourages your team to go where you lead.

Great leaders have a vision. It's easy to say you have a vision for your business: it's your life blood. You know it inside and out. Writing it down is the next step. Sharing it widely with your team is imperative too. Even more importantly, your vision for your business must provide a unifying picture so that everyone on the team, regardless of job function, can see exactly where you're going and the importance of their role in getting there. Therefore, the clearer the concept and message, the more likely you and your team can achieve the goal. Keep it short and simple.

Great leaders value their team members and create environments where they can thrive. The environment that you create is also important. Andrew Carnegie said: "You must capture and keep the heart of the original and supremely able man before his brain can do its best." When you understand what is at the core of your team members, you can serve them and allow them to reach their full potential. Value their uniqueness. Your team members are your internal customer. You must treat them at least as well as your external customer. This is the highest level of customer service. Shape the right work environment and you'll have loyal team members to lead. That means you must create a work environment that respects each person, appreciates them, and rewards their efforts and encourages an openness to change. Make it a safe environment, one which encourages trying new ideas. When you unleash personal creativity, each team member has a stake in the outcome. It's an environment that promotes growth at all levels. Combine all three elements and you have a formula for inspiring greatness and leading to breakthrough success.

Great leaders draw their teams together with clarity and consistency over time. Your team should be able to answer three questions, and it should be able to answer those three questions for everyone on the team. They include:

- What do we do?
- How do we do it?
- For whom do we do it?

As Jim Collins proved in his book, *From Good to Great*, this is not a 30-minute, one-meeting exercise; this requires 100 percent participation. It can't be a top-down decision; it must be iterative and inclusive. Great leaders tie their teams together with a unified vision and purpose. To find true and lasting success, you must become a great leader.

(KNOW) PROFIT GROWTH FACTORS

There are five profit growth factors that are important to know and prioritize.

Boost operational efficiency: The way you've always done things isn't necessarily the best way to be doing them now, and a change could give your profits a significant boost. For instance, what actually gets accomplished at those weekly meetings you hold? Try cutting back on them, freeing your time and your staff's time to spend on other income-producing tasks. If there's information all staff needs to get from you, send it to them in an email or set it up on a cloud-based document sharing system. When was the last time you inter-viewed different vendors to see if you can get better prices or terms on the inventory or raw materials you buy? Or have you asked your current vendors for better pricing? What about your merchant account provider? Your phone service? If you're still using a traditional phone line in an area with good cable or other services, you could be wasting thousands of dollars a year. Cutting your costs on recurring expenses without cutting quality gives your bottom line a nice boost. How about your inventory system? Is it automated, or is it manual, labor intensive, and prone to mistakes? While putting in inventory and order management software can be a fairly expensive project, if you do significant sales volume, the initial cost will be offset by the longer-term savings in employee time and inventory accuracy. What about all those reports your staff is creating, printing out, and handing to you? The same reports your administrative assistant later files in a filing cabinet. Do you really need them printed and filed, using up ink, toner, paper, and filing cabinet space, and therefore floor space? Could they be stored on a cloud instead? Or, for that matter, do you really need those reports at all? And what about the orders and emails they are printing out and saving in more filing cabinets as a just in case? These are just a few of the ways small businesses can increase efficiencies. One way to find inefficiencies is to write down what you are doing every day along with why you do it, the time it takes, and the result of doing the task. Ask your employees to do the same thing. Eliminate the activities that aren't necessary. Another way is to ask your employees to suggest better ways of doing the work they do.

Keep your employees happy: The process of hiring and training new employees takes time and money. Avoid that cost by doing what you can to retain your existing employees. Over the long run, having engaged, knowledgeable employees will increase your bottom line. You do not necessarily have to hand out large raises. While you should keep pay competitive, small changes like a coffee machine at work, flex time hours, a discount, or a bonus for making sales will help your employees to feel valued. If they feel valued and rewarded for their work, they are more likely to stick around.

Offer maintenance contracts: Maintenance contracts and warranties can add a healthy injection of new capital into your business. After someone buys a product, they want to know that it will work. You can reduce some of their worries by offering maintenance contracts or warranties. In addition to bringing in additional revenue for your company, this will also help to create an ongoing relationship with each client who walks into your business. Before you launch a maintenance contract program, carefully work out the numbers to be sure you charge enough for the contract so that providing services or replacements to maintenance contract customers won't put you in a money hole.

Expand to a new area: A small town may only need one café or supplement store. If your small business has already reached marketing saturation in your area, then consider expanding into a new sector. Before you decide to branch out, you will need to research the area first. How many similar businesses already exist there? What is the population density? Will overhead costs be similar to your current storefront? If you are not quite ready to set up shop in a new town, consider setting up an online storefront to sell your merchandise if you have not done so already.

Talk to your employees and customers: Your employees are your front line and connection to your customers. They have personal insight into what your customers want and current inefficiencies in your business. Ask them to share these insights. They may be able to make suggestions for new products, product changes, or ways to streamline operating processes. Make sure you personally interact with customers at some point, too. Work a cash register, answer incoming customer calls, send out surveys to customers, ask questions to find out if they are satisfied with your company's products and services. Also, be sure to ask customers to tell you what you could be doing differently and what they'd like to buy from you that you don't now sell. Their answers will help you see ways to continue to boost your business and your bottom line.

(DO) STRATEGIC PLANNING

Know these planning factors to grow, scale, and win. Let's deep dive and discuss three strategic planning avenues.

Define your business goals: Once you know where you're heading at the 30,000-foot view and what you are up against from an industry and competitive perspective, you're in a perspective to start drilling down into specific business goals that will enable you to achieve that vision. Your goals are the specific outcomes you are trying to achieve. This could include things like changes to product offerings, sales and marketing strategies, financial resources, operational efficiencies, employee culture, financial targets, and beyond. What high-level things need to happen to make your vision a reality?

Drill down to department-level objectives: As we continue to peel back the layers of the onion, we need to decide what specific objectives and initiatives we need to implement to help the company achieve each of its business goals. This is typically done department by department within the company, setting specific objectives for the product team, sales and marketing, operations, technology, finance, and human resources. For example, a business goal might be improving company morale and a specific objective of the HR department to support that goal might be to launch new employee benefits. You should limit all department-level goals to the handful of items that the department can rally around in one year. And these objects need to be made smart: specific, measurable, achievable, results-focused, and time-bound.

Determine staffing, budget, and financing needs: Once all the departmental needs have been defined and quantified, you're able to aggregate them up into one centralized company plan, organizational structure, and budget. If you don't have the full financial resources you need to achieve the plan, you have one of two choices. One, lower your targets to a level you can more easily afford, or two, raise the capital required for you to achieve your full plan.

STRATEGIC PIVOTS

Let's really get into talking about what's currently happening in the world that's affecting business. Well, it's this little round guy that has a bunch of little things on him and no one can see him called Mr. Corona. And he's making a mess of business right now. I can tell you right now, just from this last week in the companies that I work with, it has been an absolute frenzy. How do we pivot from this? How does a company that's currently selling something in the marketplace that's a novelty and doesn't have a huge online presence pivot? There are companies that were making ten million dollars a month that within a week or two dropped to almost zero, and their employees are stuck home. Additionally, they must pay salaries and other overhead costs. How do they pivot? With this mess, how do we pivot? How do our businesses survive?

Pivoting is about finding the vein of gold for you to jump into in your current business. And this looks different for different industries. But you must think of creative ways to get your product out in the marketplace because the ones that take the backburner approach on this are probably the ones who will fail in the long run. So, it's very important. In these trying times, you must own the market and drive your marketing and advertising farther than you probably ever have because the results you're trying to create now should look much different than they did before.

I know that seems probably counterintuitive, but here's the thing: if four weeks ago, there were 10,000 e-commerce stores that sold clothes, today there's probably only an eighth of that. So, what does that mean? That means now, there is more opportunity. But that's what we call risk management. I'm not telling you to take all the money out of your bank and blow it. But I'm telling you to make calculated decisions. Manage risk in a calculated way. And just don't be the other person that's used to going this way; go forward. Did Steve Jobs ever turn backwards and run the other way when he lost his company? At one point, he lost Apple. But he didn't give up; he created something to get himself back in. He took a lot of managed risk to do what he did, creating this system that we now enjoy so much and that's almost impervious to viruses. And that's how he got himself back into Apple was through that vessel: his constant innovation and creation. He created something new that put him back on the radar. But he managed risk, and he put a lot of his money into it because he knew where he wanted to be.

And the same applies to the current market. Managing fulfilment right now is key. It is ideal to plan for months of inventory if you can because if have the product and you have your core client base, you can incentivize that core client base and continue selling. What's the best way to extract money into your company? You go to your core client base and do two things. First, you ask them for more money (not literally), but you ask them to buy more product. Second, you ask them who they know who could use your product and would love it and if you can get in touch with those people to talk about your product. I know entire business models that are run that way. It's not necessarily the most scalable, but here's what it is: it's corona virus-able. It is a way. It's a way in a frenzied market where ways are limited.

Another big factor is stress mitigation, especially right now. A lot of people are feeling increased stress in their personal life. Additionally, the stress of business affects our lives because our businesses are fulfilling our life plans, and our work pays for our life plans. And if we own businesses, they are our bread and butter—our financial foundations. Some are just doing this as a hobby or part time and maybe have a j-o-b somewhere else. Well, guess what? That's in jeopardy now. So, it's key for all of us to mitigate stress. And how do we do that? Number one, stay active—your brain, your body, everything—stay engaged. And the best thing you can keep engaged in right now is keeping your business trucking forward. Stay engaged with that every single day.

I am busier in the last three weeks than I have ever been; it's crazy. But part of that is my way of managing and mitigating stress: I bury myself in the work. Do meaningful work, though, not just busy work. Do meaningful work, strategic work that takes your business farther. But I'm helping my private clients and my companies, keeping them moving forward faster, and I'm pushing them faster than ever right now. Why? While I'm going faster, everyone's going the other way, just like the stock market example. But keep yourself physically and mentally in the game. Don't check out because that's not going to help.

Additionally, there are cost cutting strategies. When we talk about delegating tasks to people, we talk about extra staff and VAs. This is where you must learn to get creative, get lean, and revamp your task delegation. Cut waste; cut it where you can. Sometimes, that's on staff, unfortunately. Sometimes, it can be systematic things that get cut. And your number one focus should be strategic pivot and sell, sell, sell, sell, fulfil, fulfil, fulfil. If you sell and fulfil right now, you'll survive. Sell the product, fulfill the product, sell it, fulfill it, sell it, fulfill it—that's it. Right now, focus on that. I'm not saying cutting costs isn't important because it is important, but until we get through this current situation, the most important thing is to sell and fulfill your product.

If you an e-commerce-based business and you have all remote employees, that changes the game a lot. When I say cut staff, you might not need to do that, but maybe you just need to cut some down to part-time. Rearrange things a little bit until we get through this time that we're going through right now. I don't know how long it's going to be; I have no idea. So, it's important to simply focus on the things that matter: support, sell, fulfill. And make sure that your customer support is spot on and that your clients love you to death because of it. It should always be that way, but unfortunately, it's not always that way. But it's always a good time to focus on that.

Another important focus is strategic realignment, if possible. The first step is to pivot to own the market share. How do you pivot to own the market share? Simple. Keep driving the car forward, not backwards, and start investing more into your company, more into your product, more into getting it in front of as many eyeballs as you possibly can. Why? Because fewer people are doing that. Your competition is dwindling by the day because they're pulling back because of fear and uncertainty. And that's the worst mistake you can make. The second step is to figure out what your unique USP is. If you don't have one, you need to create one. What makes you different, especially right now? Figure out what makes your unique. What is it that you do that's unique and that all these other people used to do, and now, you can soak up the market share for them? I don't have the answer for each of your individual businesses, but it's your product. You should know that. Be creative.

This is where that strategic you, the visionary you, must come out and put the time and effort into thinking through all the aspects of your business. I frequently rent a hotel room and lock myself in a room for a weekend to dive into strategic thought. I just sit there and write stuff down on paper. Half of it is garbage at the end, but guess what? One or two awesome things come out of that time. Again, be creative with this. You can use a white board or paper. Lock yourself away and brainstorm. How can I be different? How can I be unique in this business? That may change your avatar, but it's important to figure out what makes your business special and unique. Focus on that unique USP as part of your marketing. And if you do that, the results you'll see will be far different from the results you've had in the past.

CHAPTER 3

DELEGATED OUTCOMES,

LEADERSHIP, AND PROFIT

MAXIMIZATION

Let's dive into the heartbeat and meaningful scoreboard for your business. You've probably heard the saying, "What gets measured gets managed." And that is true when it comes to anything that you do in business. If you are not measuring it, you cannot manage it. So that's the heartbeat of your business—your scorecard, your numbers. It is vital to measure, and manage, your numbers.

Earlier in the book, we talked about leadership and how leadership principles are important in business. This comes with the culture, how you lead, how you manage, all of that is very, very key to the success of any organization. It doesn't matter what that organization is, if it's a non-profit, for-profit, or rec center. If you have employees, and it's an employee-based model or even a contractor-based model. It's very important to manage and lead your team in the most effective way. And we'll talk about a few different ways that you can do that.

Leadership is not about a position. There are many different types of leaders. Some leaders are dictators; others are too passive, so you have both ends of the spectrum. What you want to try to focus on is being a leader that's right in the center, in the center of it all. I like to use the terms firm, fair, and consistent. Every leader should strive to be firm, fair, and consistent. Leadership is not about a position; it's about a behavior. It is important that you act and behave like the leader of an organization. A great principle to follow is to lead by example. However, I like to use a little different terminology, and that's influence by example. Because at the end of the day, getting people to do the things we want them to do is all about influence. It's how we influence them to get the job done in the most efficient and effective way that affects every single piece of our business.

Another important focus of a leader is meaningful impacts. We must have an impact on the people that we lead. So, we have to have a meaningful impact on everybody that we work with in our company. That includes our executive suite, the people who are under us, and everyone in our company.

Up next is action, action, action. Not words. Don't be the do as I say, not as I do type of leader. It's very important that leaders lead from the front. It doesn't matter what company model you have, you just lead from the front, and people will inherently mimic you. I can tell you from years of experience in the military that good leaders have good followers, and as a leader, you must know how to be a follower first. And don't be afraid to admit your mistakes. Mistakes happen to everyone; all of us make mistakes. We all make mistakes in our businesses, in our personal lives, in many different facets of our lives, not just in business.

But what's important as a CEO of a company or a leader of a company is that we're not afraid because most of the time that's what ends up holding us back— fear. We're fear driven. Instead of letting fear drive us, we want to focus on leading from the front, and when we make a mistake, we don't push that onto a subordinate as if it was their fault. I've seen this too many times with companies that I've worked with in the past, where leaders didn't take responsibility for their actions and admit they were wrong. When you do that, it costs you something—respect. And respect is huge. Respect is not something that is given; it's earned. It's very much earned.

And lastly, it's all about your people. Unity equals strength. When you come together as a company and the culture is there as a single unit, that is unity and strength. It creates that unity and strength, and your company then, in turn, ends up having this beautifully designed bond. Some companies do a great job at building this. They have daycare centers built right into them. They have flex hours. These are all things that promote this unity and strength and cohesiveness inside of that company. Company culture is an important aspect of your business. And if you run a business but don't have employees, it is still important to become a self-guided leader. You should still provide yourself the same leadership as if you had a full staff of employees. Always look at it that way, as I lead from the front. I am the direct reflection of my company's mission and vision. When you're those things and you have that clarity in your company, that's when you can design, from a leadership standpoint, a company that has good synergy and a good company culture.

And that's one thing I've always been very proud of in the past with many of my companies is one of the big compliments I've always gotten is I love to work here because there's good synergy and we're allowed to run with the ball. That is empowerment. I love to empower people. You'll get your best results when you empower others.

Another important aspect is to know delegated outcomes. Earlier I talked about the importance of delegation. Delegation is a repeated theme because it's such a huge piece of the puzzle. But now we're going to talk about delegated outcomes. Many leaders or executive staff depend on the fire-and-forget model. And it never works. It's not efficient. You can't fire and forget a delegated task. Therefore, it's not only the task that is delegated but also the outcome. You're delegating a task, but you're also delegating an outcome alongside of it.

My philosophy is that I don't care how you go from A to Z, but I know the outcome that I want. Here's the task; how you skin that onion in the middle, as long as you're going to get to the required outcome, doesn't matter. This brings us back to empowerment. You empower people to do the things that you want them to do, and you don't have to micromanage. Accountability is vital. If we hold people accountable for tasks, our outcomes will be better. There are lots of things you can do inside of this model with incentive programs, but no matter how you do it, holding people accountable for tasks and outcomes is extremely important.

The one thing I really hate is micromanagement. I can't stand micromanagers. It's usually not at the executive level where you have an issue with micromanagement. It's usually down at second and third levels of leadership where you run into a lot of problems when it comes to micromanagement. It's usually a big stumbling block in a lot of companies at lower levels. So how do you get rid of this in a company? Sometimes, it comes right back to the principles that you're modeling. How you act directly affects how they act, so you must consider that.

Your behavior, how you train your staff, what you model, and how you lead all affect lower-level leaders in your company.

Lastly, you must expect ownership. Ownership is huge. When we delegate a task to someone else, we want them to feel like they own it; it's theirs. They own the task and feel responsible for it. They know that they're the one in charge of not only the task but also the outcome. And we should empower people to do that. And we expect our leaders to have that ownership in the process of completing tasks, whether those are daily tasks, monthly tasks, or yearly tasks. However they support the company, they should always strive for excellence.

Next, we'll dive into profit maximization. There are three simple principles of profit maximization. And those principles are:

- Increase sales and revenue while we hold cost constant
- Decrease cost while holding sales and revenue constant
- A combination of the two: increase or decrease the input or output model

If I go back to the input/output model that we talked about, you want to focus on small inputs with large outputs. These are the key things that you're doing in your company that are profit generating inputs. So those inputs go in, they create a large output, which is a larger amount of cash flow. And this is more of the mid-term approach. Or you can flip this model over, where you have large inputs and small outputs. You're still going to create cash flow if you do this strategically, but this approach changes the formula around for time because you must focus on tactical inputs. You're not after today money.

Strategical inputs create more mid-term and long-term profits. But, depending on how your business runs, you can decrease or increase that input or output model.

Deep Dive on Technology/Systems/ Process/SOPs

Other important aspects of running your business efficiently include technology, systems, processes, and SOPs. Areas of focus include the environment of success, the aim and target, process = SOPs = WRR (Wash, Rinse, and Repeat), and the correct inputs. The outcome will be predictable and stable systems and processes. You'll learn to build your own "environment of success" and inputs that create more profits in your business.

The environment of success is like an ecosystem. That is the whole systematic piece of this that makes your whole process work and work smoothly. This is another area of your business that is affected by your input and the choices you make regarding input. Acquisition on the front end creates the profit. That entire small action creates a big result, right? So that's the true growth and scalability. Knowing your best plug-ins is huge. For your widget that you are selling, know where to get your customer from and target that in the right way. Where does your target hang out? What is that group of people? Where do they hang out online? Where do they hang out offline? How do you effectively target that as a best plug-in for the acquisition phase? So, you know your ideal customer, and you know where to get them. Examples of this include cold calling, B2B, door to door, and sales reps. It all depends on what your structure is in your company and the best avenue of approach to acquire that front-end customer or lead that turns into a customer.

Next is the sales process in the environment of success. Solid feeds through the acquisition process into the sales pipeline are critical because once we get them into that pipeline, we can push into that pipeline and tweak the performance of that pipeline as we go. And this is where you must ensure that you master the systems and process that you're working with so you can effectively manipulate that process. As you go through, tweak the performance for its peak performance to ensure that you're squeezing every single dollar out of that system and process through your sales pipeline. No matter what, all of this must be duplicatable across everything in your company, throughout every widget, throughout every continuity program, whether it's service-based or an actual physical product. This process must be duplicatable across every single area of your company and every product.

And then the output, that's the profit generator so we must make sure that we're getting that good profit coming out through the inputs, process, sales process, into the output. And then it's into the feedback. That's always ROI generating, and most importantly, we're creating re-investable cash flow back through the feedback loop to continue to scale and grow the company.

Throughout the entire process, we're focusing on leveraging all aspects of our business. Therefore, we've leveraged everything to this point to create large profits for us. And all of this should be systematic and programmed. None of this should be done manually. And it's all oriented into that feedback loop where you have a percentage set aside to put back in the company. You set that percentage for yourself, but let's say that for every dollar that comes through this process that's profit, you take 25 percent and roll that right back into the set aside, which brings us to the feedback loop.

The set aside is the reinvestment. This process is the recycling and reinvesting back into your company because the only way you're going to scale your company monetarily is if you recycle a portion of that dollar and reinvest it back into growth. So, we must identify those places that are giving us a great ROI, and we put some of that reinvested money back into those places where ROI is the biggest. This is how ensure profit splits. Regardless of how this looks for you, you must know your pots of money so you can sufficiently scale the company in the correct way. This reinvestment process is how you create growth and scale in unison. That's important. It's easy to scale, but if we don't do the growth and scale pieces together, one part will outpace the other.

To review, we start with input. Input could be advertising, sales, or other things. Next is the process itself—the sales pipeline, which leads to your output. And then from there, we're going to lead this into what I call the feedback loop, which is your reinvestment. Reinvest to increase ROI. And then it's simply wash, rinse, and repeat. You're going to hear me say that a million times: wash, rinse, and repeat because that's what we want to do. We want to reinvest a certain amount through this feedback loop back into this input to continue to feed this process repeatedly. It's a constant loop. We want to continue to do that to scale, scale, scale. And with that is grow, grow, grow. And again, growth and scale together are vital.

Overall, it's a very simple process. But you must decide what your feedback percentage is. Is that a 25 percent reinvestment?

Is that a 30 percent reinvestment? What does that look like for you? You need to decide what it is.

Let's hop into the next speed exercise. Again, you have one minute to knock out this speed exercise; don't put a whole lot of thought into this. I want you to take this as raw as you can, right off the top of your head, right now in this very moment. Think about what three positives in your environment of success are that you have right and then three negatives in your environment of success that you currently have wrong. Hold yourself accountable to one minute.

(BE) LEADERSHIP

Are you interested in growing as a leader or just in getting ahead? In my experience as a leader, I see a lot of people who want to advance. Only caring about yourself and your advancement as a business owner likely will not get you very far. Let's talk about some opportunities to grow as a leader. The more closely you follow them, the better your chances of success.

Identify your motivation. How you feel about yourself starts with how motivated you are. It takes self-motivation to remove the obstacles that keep you from developing and growing, and ultimately, all motivation is self-motivation. Before you can grow as a leader, you must know the why behind your drive. Once you do, you will know the way.

Unmask your flaws. To conquer your flaws, you must first accept them. Once you know your weaknesses, no one else can use them against you, and you're better prepared to grow as a leader. Everyone has flaws, but when you understand yours, you can embrace who you are. Learn from your failures.

Growing as a leader means developing the ability and willingness to have your failures shape you. Failure is instructive. It allows you, as a leader, to learn. We all fall. But failure means we refuse to get back up and deal with our issues.

Appreciate feedback. No one likes hearing that they've done something wrong, but try to view all feedback as a gift, an opportunity to develop. The best leaders realize feedback helps them improve so they can do better. We all need people in our lives who can give us feedback. Seek it with sincerity and receive it with grace.

Listen to those with more experience. Listen to the experienced people in your life, not because they're always right but because they have a better understanding of being wrong. To grow in wisdom, you need to pay attention to those who have experience. They can teach you to listen when you want to speak, to stop and think when you want to react, to keep trying when you want to quit, and each of those little steps will help you grow into a great leader.

Refuse to settle and be mediocre. Don't allow your fears to limit you to become mediocre. If you want to pursue excellence, it takes hard work. If you want to go beyond what's expected, you must evolve and grow to advance and make progress. The best leaders, the ones who really want to grow, never settle for being mediocre. They understand that good enough is just not good enough.

Invest in yourself. If you're truly interested in growing, create an environment in which you can invest in yourself so you can be at your best. Make time to read. Surround yourself with clever people and experts. Investing in yourself pays high dividends because when you feel good about yourself you are more motivated to work hard and succeed and grow.

At the end of the day, you'll take one of two paths as a leader: either you'll step forward into growth or backward into safety. The choice will be yours.

(KNOW) PROFIT GROWTH FACTORS

Where do the most successful companies look for profit growth strategy inspiration? Not at their competitors. Not at the market. And not necessarily at even their customers. They're searching for insights within their sales transaction data. Most companies have millions of transactions to dig through. The overwhelming nature of this task leads to procrastination, analysis mistakes, and the overwhelming feeling of not knowing where to begin. So, let's break down a few shortcuts.

Identify price increases failing to cover cost increases by customer. Overall, finding price increases failing to overset overall costs is easy. The more important insights are hidden within customer data. To evaluate this data accurately, you first need to isolate price, volume, cost, and mix changes. This allows your team to compare price to cost and get a true picture of how the relationship between them shake out by customer and prioritize the area of opportunity quickly and effectively. Don't settle for the common but dangerous attitude of, "There's nothing we can do." When you find situations in which your prices haven't covered your costs, this is your opportunity to fix this problem and see margins bounce back as quickly as possible. Instead, build a plan to slowly but firmly increase prices over the next year, learning from the places you have been successful. Also identify through sales transaction analysis. To support these efforts, consider emphasizing adding value and working to enhance product mix for each affected customer. If you simply can't change your prices, adjust your offering instead. Reduce value-added perks such as same-day customer service or shipping and tracking. As soon as your customers understand the loss, they will often feel more inclined to pay the higher price. Even if they don't, you've still balanced out your pricing relative to value, boosting your potential for profit growth.

Determine which sales reps sell at the lowest prices. Many sales incentive plans are built around volume alone—a common but critical mistake. So, it's not surprising that sales reps follow this lead and take drastic price-cutting measures to sell more product. This has obvious negative implications for margins, but until the system changes, they have little motivation to sell on higher price points. First, find the biggest offenders and address the problem head-on. Use profit waterfall analysis to determine which sales reps dilute prices through discounts, allowances, and rebates the most often and at the highest levels. Don't forget to drill down further into the data to evaluate your team members by customer, markets, and products. You may find a sales rep gives away allowances only to keep a major company happy. Or the rep could struggle selling a specific product and resort to price cutting instead of selling on value. Help each team member get to the root of these problems to build a strategy to overcome them. Once you understand the biggest issues at play, update your incentive plans accordingly to reward more suitable and profitable behavior. For example, if one sales rep struggles in a specific market, reward his or her success in sustaining high prices in this market. Supplement these incentive programs with coaching to help your sales team proactively identify areas of opportunity. Sales management should work with the team, not against them. Incentives alone are not enough. Active coaching on pricing is critical.

Identify your least profitable customers. Using the profit waterfall analysis, we discussed above, shift focus to your customers. Factor in all discounts, allowances, and rebates to gain an accurate view of profitability via account. Which customers cost you the least and therefore impact your margins positively? Which cost the most and therefore provide narrow margins—if any at all? Using these insights, work on a two-part strategy. First, evaluate your most expensive customers first to determine how to manage them effectively. Focus on slowly but firmly raising prices by emphasizing value. If these customers agree to pay more, you've directly improved your margins. If they leave for a competitor, you've still eliminated a drain on your resources that wasn't delivering profits anyway. Any outcome results in a win of profit growth. Then, evaluate your low-cost customer delivering higher prices. What separates these customers from the high-cost ones? What lessons can you learn from these differences? Apply these lessons learn and profitable strategies to your high-cost customers to build a sustainable revenue strategy for this year and outline years to come.

(DO) Strategic Planning

If you subscribe to the notion that leaders do the strategic planning and staff execute it, then getting buy-in from the people who will make the plan come to life is critical. There are a few ways for leaders to engage staff, so they feel included in the process without letting the strategy development execution process get out of hand. With this sure-fire approach, you'll be on the right track.

First, run some paid working lunch sessions with staff where you blow up the strategy map, post it on a conference room wall, and ask groups of your staff to place sticky notes on the themes or objectives where they see their daily work fitting into the strategy. If employees have a hard time finding where they fit in, it can spark a useful, in-depth conversation about the strategy map and objectives. Additionally, it may help reveal some areas where staff may be spending time on a project that is not important to long-term strategy of the organization. Use this exercise as a start point. Once the enterprise strategic plan is complete, managers and supervisors should ensure that all employees understand the strategy map and scorecard.

Second, the second step begins as you ask your staff to create their personal strategic plans. To create their personal strategic plans, staff should select three to five objectives from the enterprise strategic map they feel they can help the organization achieve. They should aim to keep it balanced across the four perspectives of the map, and they should establish cause and effect relationships between their contribution and the strategic results sought by the organization. To do this, they should develop personal objectives that align to the organization's objective and the measures and targets they will use to determine whether they are achieving their objectives.

Once employees have developed this personal scorecard, they should have a conversation with their supervisors to assure it aligns to the goals of the organization and is within the employee's influence. This exercise will both enable staff to contribute to the strategy management framework and establish their connection to their entire enterprise strategy.

If you want to engage staff and keep them engaged during the strategic planning process, continue these conversations and have regular check-ins. Make sure they know the strategic plan will not be something that gets put on the shelf and forgotten about and neither will their personal strategic plan. Since employees will be executing your strategic plan, whether you engage staff may very well make or break your work strategy.

STRATEGIC PIVOTS

Let's discuss four ways that you can pivot your business.

Change competitive positioning and pricing to improve traction. When we look at this, many high margin, low volume businesses are focused to consider the price-volume tradeoff. Of course, a move on price also puts them in the realm of new competitors including e-commerce vendors and big box stores. You can't be on both ends of the spectrum at the same time.

Consider alternative technology platforms for the solution. Sometimes, businesses have to pivot to a new technology to stay competitive or improve margins. Other domains like transportation have found the need to pivot to meet environmental directives and alternative forms of energy. The world around us is changing quickly, even for businesses that have been operating for fifty or sixty years.

Adapt to emerging customer need or pain. As economic conditions change and government regulations evolve, businesses are motivated to seek new tools and processes for risk reduction and continued growth. It can be extremely valuable to pivot the focus of your new software technology tool from productivity to compliance.

Position your business as a social enterprise, not a commercial enterprise. I see many young businesses with a passion primarily for social change who don't realize that changing the world costs money. The best are able to keep their social focus while pivoting their business strategy to make money. These two objectives are not mutually exclusive. To me, a pivot is as natural in a start-up as seeking outside funding or shuffling executive roles to better match founder strengths and weaknesses. You don't wait for a crisis to start thinking about it. And you need not hide your pivots for fear of showing weakness. The sooner you recognize the need to make a change, the less it costs and the greater the return. Why are you still hesitating?

PART 2
PUBLIC RELATIONS

CHAPTER 4

PUBLIC RELATIONSHIP

MANAGEMENT

Many companies actively engage in issues management. This involves analyzing the news and developing communication strategies around pertinent issues and trends. Then, they communicate their messages through the media.

Effective communication goes beyond managing issues via the media. Companies and organizations need to be aware of the external public, people, and groups outside their organization's sphere and that can affect or are affected by what they do.

This is called relationship management. This is the art of identifying key people and creating strategies to build and maintain mutually beneficial relationships.

You are likely already using media monitoring to monitor the issues that impact your company, just like most companies. You might even go one step further by conducting media analysis. This includes assigning tones such as neutral, negative, or positive to news stories. If you aren't, you should. Your communications team won't do its job well if it doesn't perform properly without proper analysis and evaluation.

It's when you add another dimension to your existing monitoring and analytics that it becomes interesting. This is best illustrated by tracking and analyzing quotes. Tracking quotes helps you identify your key publics. It allows you to see what your key publics are thinking, saying, and doing.

You can identify the type and nature of relationships between your organization's key stakeholders by making small adjustments, such as using quotes to cross-reference tone with quotes. This will allow you to see what is working and what isn't, and help you develop a plan for changing the relationship.

The odds of someone being quoted as an ally in a positive cause are higher if the article or quote is positive. Contrarily, the more negative a quote or article is, the higher the likelihood that they are opposed to issues favorable for your organization.

The more times someone is quoted, the higher the likelihood that they are an opinion leader. This is a person who knowingly or unknowingly influences opinion. Your organization should strive to have a professional and open dialogue with opinion leaders, regardless of their position.

Many people believe that the media is ultimately responsible for shaping public opinion. While they have a lot of influence, they are just one piece in the PR puzzle. It is important that PR professionals don't limit themselves to the media. It's sometimes best to get right to the source when possible. As a professional communicator, you have one primary job: to communicate information. Not necessarily to deal directly with the media. It doesn't matter how you get the information out to your audiences. What matters is that they receive the information. Writing news releases and using the media are just means to an end.

Over 61% of Americans belong or are members of a group or organization. This includes professional associations, religious groups, unions, and organizations. These groups are made up of opinion leaders.

After identifying the opinion leaders and groups, it is important to create consistent messages that clearly communicate your organization's position on key issues. You run the risk of appearing hypocritical or insincere if you don't have consistency. It is not a good idea to communicate different messages about the same topic.

Consistency is key to building trust with people and your organization. Building trust is the first step to building a relationship between the opinion leaders, and the key publics.

Honesty is the best policy in all communications. It is dangerous to try and manipulate the media or the public. People might not like everything you say but they will believe you and be more respectful of you over time.

Organizations can monitor the media to make sure everyone is following the same message. This helps to avoid misunderstandings due to inadvertent contradictions and aggressive spokespersons. Proactive media analysis allows you to gauge the acceptance of your organization's position by key publics and other influential people, such as media.

Media analysis can be used to identify miscommunications and the root cause. It can also be used to identify key opinion leaders and publics and determine their position on a particular issue. It is important to remember that relationship managing involves dealing directly with people. Media analysis is a tool that helps ensure your organization communicates honestly and effectively. The media are only a medium for communicating your message.

Even if your media analysis program is top-notch, you must still communicate with your key audiences to find out their views on key issues and how your organization is perceived by them. Public relations and communications are all about effective communication. Nothing is better than direct contact with the source.

Public relations are a key factor in how your business is perceived by the public. It's the relationship between your company and customers, past customers, and community members, as well as potential customers.

Two ways to get PR are possible. Press releases are a way to share information about achievements or events within your company. This PR allows you to control how your company is perceived by the public. Your public is any person or entity that has an interest in your business, such as employees, customers, suppliers, and competitors. Your perception of yourself by the public can have a significant impact on your business's future.

Make sure the information in your press release is relevant to the readers and viewers of the publication. The headline of your press release should grab readers' attention and encourage them to read on. You should target publications that would be interested in your information. If you send a press release on Christmas ornaments to a publication that is focused on outdoor life, it will not be a success.

When you need to overcome objections and build credibility, case histories, and demonstrate customer satisfaction with your products and company, testimonials and case histories can be very useful. A press release should not include testimonials. While it is nice to include a testimonial from a customer who has been satisfied, ensure that the comment is directly related to the main point of your press release.

A good reputation from satisfied customers can help you build a large customer base. However, one negative review from a customer can do serious damage to your business. In a one-on-1 meeting, your customer should speak most of the words. Customers are worth listening to, and valuable feedback is invaluable information. Listen to what they have to say and take the time to learn about their needs. This will allow you to provide the best service possible. Your customers will feel pressured and turned off if you do most of the talking. You also run the risk of losing a sale.

Promoting your business and building a strong customer base is important. It's essential to build a relationship with the public. Keeping in touch with customers will improve customer relations and help keep you in mind of prospects and customers.

A business's most valuable asset is its clients. Without clients, there is no business. If clients are not of high quality, business will suffer. However, if you can get good clients and keep them loyal, your business will continue to grow. All this sounds great. It is difficult to find good clients, and even more challenging to keep them. Your competition may be trying to do the same thing and using better methods to win business. What innovative ways can you build client relationships?

This discussion is about direct sales and not selling merchandise to large consumers. If you are a contractor who maintains air conditioners at clients' workplaces, this is an example. You could also be a direct seller to business buyers of computer hardware, or any other businesses that have large sales to individual customers.

Client satisfaction is the first requirement. Pricing may be secondary if the client is happy with your after-sales service, response time and confidence in you. Clients won't buy from suppliers whose prices are the lowest. You are on the right track if your product costs only a small portion of your client's total expenses, or your product is vital for them. How can you retain these clients in the face of all the competition? What other factors are important than client satisfaction?

Another important factor is the relationship. Are you able to relate to your clients professionally or as good friends? These extremes can be damaging. Good friendship is not good for your business's long-term health. Your business will be directly affected by any problem in your personal friendship. What if your client relationships were purely professional? The answer is right in front of you.

A relationship that is not based on friendships but also takes a mechanical approach to the problem is what is required. It is important to strike a balance between professional and personal relationships.

CHAPTER 5

WRITING A PRESS RELEASE

Online marketers are always on the lookout for promotional channels that are novel and are yet to be saturated with the unfortunate stigma of marketing abuse. Different people are constantly trying to find new ways by which they could promote their online enterprises.

One of the newer, and most effective, marketing strategies are press releases. Press releases are informative and objective pieces which are supposed to be newsworthy and are circulated in PR wires for pickup by various news groups and editors. Once a press release is picked up, it can be published in various channels all over the Internet, or even through print publications.

Immediately, the sharp marketing mind would be able to see the grand potentials of press releases as amazing tools that would help them spread the word about their business. Imagine the promising things that await if ever a press release is picked up or print or online publication. Such would be tantamount to instantaneous exposure for your business to entirely new audiences.

However, you cannot simply write a press release the same way you would an article, or a content piece, or a sales letter. To employ the same style with press releases would be to court disaster. Your press release won't be accepted by newswires; hence, it won't have the chance to get picked up.

So how exactly should you write a press release? Let's look at the guidelines below.

- Pay attention to the 5 Ws. These are Who, What, When, Where, and Why. These are the questions which your press release should focus on. If you're going to write a press release for your dog grooming business, for example, you should be able to state who you are, what your business is about, when it will, or was, launched, where it can be found and why it was established. If you are going to launch, or just launched, a new product, you would have to state who the creator is, what the product is all about, when it was or will be launched, where it can be bought, and why it was introduced to the market.
- Be objective. Remember, a press release should be a newsworthy item. News is never subjective. Stay away from flowery words that merely tend to hype up what you want to discuss. Stick with the facts, and only the facts. You are writing news, not a promotional piece.
- The ultimate aim is to promote your product but to be subtle about it. To do this, reorient your focus. Try to make your press release informative instead of persuasive. Remember, you're not writing a sales copy. You're writing something that would announce your business or your product.
- There are three parts to a press release: the headline, the summary, and the body. The headline is the title of your piece. The summary is a paragraph that

would serve as an introduction to your press release, or a summary of its most salient contents. The body is where you objectively discuss the 5 Ws.

- Length is not a factor. Don't ever think that if you write a longer press release, it will have a better chance of getting picked up. Often, the rule is, the more concise your press release, the better its chances are of success. A 1,000-word piece is considered a little too lengthy for a press release. Around 300 to 700 words are succinct enough for this purpose.

Press releases can win for your business the exposure it needs. It is capable of instantaneous results for as long your press release gets picked up and published. A lot of Internet marketers have testified to the power of press releases as marketing tools. So put on your thinking cap and commence to write an objective and informative piece about your business or product, observe the guidelines we have delineated above, and ready yourself for the new audience you're most certain to garner.

CASE STUDY 1
TECH SVY INC. HAS HUGE
GROWTH IN THEIR MARKET

The company's business saw a sudden decline in sales and market share, but with our help they were able to recover within just months. This turnaround strategy combined renewed commitment from top management across departments as well as fresh branding that was planned cross-functionally for the first time ever.

REALIZED GROWTH

Staffing over a 3-month period: 80%

Revenue growth over a 3-month period: 240% increase

THE PIVOT

Tech SVY Inc., under our guidance, had been focused on profits over brand equity. The company reoriented itself to focus primarily in the industry's core and promoted its own brands, eliminating weak resellers while also promoting stronger ones from other companies through advertising campaigns that enabled them be noticed by more customers than ever before.

OUR APPROACH IN SEGMENTS

We are focusing on the essentials. Our core brand and our most fundamental offerings will take priority over other projects for this year to best serve you as customers with an eye toward long-term success

With our strategic planning services, we helped companies of all shapes and sizes find their voice. From developing coordinated brand strategies that allowed cross-functional groups to channel media spending toward the company's own message; crafting tailored campaigns for each client based on what they wanted rather than just a "one size fits all" approach. This is how integrated communications can make your business grow.

The only way to get ahead in this competitive market is by taking a new approach. Partnering up with others who share your values and interests will help you stay on top.

The launch of a new brand is always an exciting event. It's the first time that people get to experience what you have created, and this can lead them down their own path, exploring all your products or services for themselves.

The brand ambassador program is the perfect opportunity to make your company's products and services known. This can be done through personal sales, word-of-mouth advertising, or just by creating an engaging social media presence that will draw people in who may not have heard of you before. The relatable tone should stay consistent across all communication channels, so it feels like one big family reunion where everyone knows how much they've always loved each other but now finally realize what a great thing fate had planned out for them when she brought these two together at this moment.

CASE STUDY 2
LMV MERCHANT CO. FINDS NEW AVENUES TO SUSTAINED PROFITABILITY

The LMV Merchant Co. needed to increase profitability and identified four key areas for cutting costs. Analysis showed that by reducing these expenditures, they would be able achieve a greater revenue over the 4-month period as compared with previous years—and it worked.

REALIZED GROWTH

Staffing over a 6-month period: 125%

Revenue growth over a 4-month period: 125% increase

THE PIVOT

LMV Merchant Co., one of the top 25% players in the industry, operates in a scale-driven industry that was showing early signs of price pressure. This pressure was already affecting profits.

Planning and decision-making have traditionally been made with a significant emphasis on "gut feel" with little actual testing or research.

This often leads to sub-optimal outcomes, as decision-makers are not taking into account all of the relevant information. A more data-driven approach would help in making informed decisions.

By working with LMV Merchant Co., our goal was to help the company identify cost savings and revenue growth opportunities for them be profitable. We also provided rigor to their decision-making process so they could stay competitive within their market space.

OUR APPROACH IN SEGMENTS

To identify cost-saving opportunities, we used process improvement strategies and methods that were fact based. Our indepth analysis of the operation revealed many areas where improvements could be made to save money for our company while still providing excellent customer service.

- Digital advertising and call-center operations

- Purchase

- Logistics

- Business processes

- Organizational structures

- Back-office functions

Our analysis revealed four areas that could lead to improved profitability in the near, medium, and long-term. These included cost-reduction measures as well as business process improvements. This will help them achieve their goals of becoming more profitable by adopting new technologies or methods for accomplishing work cheaply without sacrificing quality workmanship.

An additional potential avenue was globalization: opening international markets so they don't only service American clients but also provide goods overseas service, also.

CASE STUDY 3
SOLAR SENSE INC. PRICED GOODS CORRECTLY AND THEIR CUSTOMERS RESPONDED

Solar Sense, Inc.'s strategy was to compete on price but changing market conditions forced them into an arms race where they had to increase prices to maintain profitability. This created a problem for customers who were no longer able to buy because their profits had also decreased.

We developed our own model that took region-specific factors such as customer base size and power output needs into account so we could offer more tailored solutions, which proved effective.

REALIZED GROWTH

Staffing over a 5-month period: 150%

Revenue growth over a 5-month period: 175% increase

THE PIVOT

To remain competitive, Solar Sense Inc. had no choice but to adapt as market conditions changed and their internal structure became more complex. With their expertise, Solar Sense Inc. has become one of the most trusted names in solar technologies. They offer a quick time-to-market for innovations and installations that are affordable to everyone.

As the market for Solar panels became more competitive, prices dropped, and customers responded by refusing to sign long-term contracts. They asked that indexing be done when decreases in average costs occured so they could enjoy savings on their terms.

These are some of the reasons why customers were dissuaded from considering Solar Sense Inc. as a solution to their solar needs:

High price assurance contracts tied discounting and sale prices with an underlying cost index decreasing over time. This strategy discouraged potential buyers by making them think about how much money they would have spent investing in other solutions like panels or batteries, which did not offer discounts but had lower upfront investment costs

The company has found it challenging to respond promptly and creatively when faced with changes in its pricing strategy. To address this issue, we were asked by the management team to assist them in developing new approaches for dynamic market penetration and a cohesive system. Of course, this would work best within current conditions like an "adaptive" or interactive model where they can test different strategies until one proves successful enough without going too far down any paths just yet.

OUR APPROACH IN THIS SITUATION

We helped Solar Sense Inc. create a new pricing strategy by taking apart their old model. We also developed multiple methods for market penetration, which were based on facts and data rather than guessing as before. This is all because C-Suite guidance conversations allowed us to work with executives from different departments towards achieving company goals together.

CASE STUDY 4
DIGI CONSULTING LTD.
CREATES FIRST CLASS DIRECT
MARKETING THROUGH
TESTING DESIGN

When many companies are feeling increasingly competitive, Digi Consulting Ltd. wanted to increase its share of high-value clients. We collaborated with them on creating experimentally designed direct marketing campaigns that increased response rates and improved profitability for all parties involved.

REALIZED GROWTH

Staffing over a 4-month period: 10%

Revenue growth over a 6-month period: 150% increase

THE PIVOT

Digi Consulting Ltd. has been facing increased competition from a saturated market of providers over the past few years. However, they had experienced significant growth through capitalizing on new markets and hiring us to increase their share in high-value clientele by retaining more customers as well as winning back those lost during this time frame due primarily because we were able to experiment with direct marketing campaigns, which may help them achieve these goals faster than anticipated before costs were incurred.

OUR APPROACH IN SEGMENTS

With the help of data analytics, we were able to model what would happen if our product was improved or changed. Using fractional factorial analysis instead of traditional A/B testing methods allowed us to test different variables to find out which ones have the most impact on customer response rates without uncertainty.

A second analytical tool was created to project the financial impact on all offer combinations. The Net Present Value (NPV) model was based on Digi Consulting LTD. finances and used both observed conversion rates as input and modeled responses at each level for an accurate forecast of revenue potentials that can be achieved through direct marketing campaigns with different scopes or sizes—from small local businesses up to significant chains such as Walmart and Target.

This allows marketers to test new ideas without spending too much money beforehand to get valuable insights into what works best before investing heavily into production planning.

The marketing agency discovered that certain variables caused customers to respond more often than others. For example, offers with three or four times as many responses generated an original offer, and high price points did not seem appealing.

Using our advanced analytics marketing capabilities, Digi Consulting LTD. was able to identify the most profitable direct campaign for rollout nationwide. We also helped them develop in-house expertise and conduct multivariate campaigns that were more successful than those before it with better results across various channels such as email or social media engagement rates per post.

We're passionate about helping companies grow by finding out what works best when running digital advertising, not just how much you can spend but where your money should go to have maximum impact on customer acquisition.

CASE STUDY 5
WATER PURE TVT INC.
PERFORMS AN OPERATIONAL
MODEL OVERHAUL THAT
KICKSTARTS SALES

Water Pure TVT Inc. is reviving growth and scaling by focusing on customers and expanding its front line. Unrealized cash flow was possible by plugging in new markets and B2B consumers.

REALIZED GROWTH

Staffing over an 8-month period: 400%

Revenue growth over a 5-month period: 500% increase

THE PIVOT

With our approach, the sales team provided data-driven insights into their customers. This included patterns of behavior and unmet needs that were unique for each client to make tailored solution recommendations based on what they need most at this time—all thanks to some helpful new technology from Water Pure TVT Inc. With our help, Water Pure TVT Inc. was able to reorganize its operations to serve each customer better, thus increasing profits dramatically.

OUR APPROACH IN SEGMENTS

For any business to grow, you need the right levers. For example, Water Pure TVT Inc. was having difficulty winning new clients and maximizing their value with existing ones—so they reached out for help from us. Our team designed an integrated approach that would target specific audiences based on where potential business could come from (e.g., cold calling vs. online advertising). We also helped them identify what messages were most effective at getting prospects into buying mode. It's been a resounding success since our work started.

Water Pure TVT Inc.'s sales efforts were inefficient. To find gaps in their distribution network, they analyzed customers by geography: consumer B2C and commercial builders/renovators, etc., finding no coverage for new construction projects from any one group alone.

The first step was analyzing Water Pure TVT Inc.'s customer base by segmenting them into different categories such as geographic regions, such as domestic vs. international. This process allowed us to discover what opportunities could have been missed out. Only certain groups' representatives had access to information about prospective clients, while others did not.

With data from new housing starts and commercial activity, we were able to show the company how realigning its sales resources could help it target markets more effectively. We didn't just re-assign customer accounts. Instead, our insights included information about specific behavior patterns in each market as well as unmet needs that Water Pure TVT Inc. was addressing.

Our approach was successful because it utilized relevant metrics such as residential or business revenues, which allowed us an accurate measure against other companies' performance.

For Water Pure TVT Inc., we identified an analytical model to calculate each customer's full potential. This analysis was performed by product category and location to determine where they had the most significant opportunity to grow their business.

Based on attributes of satisfied customers fully served, Water Pure TVT Inc. attentively listened to what was needed regarding their services, taking action through importation into their CRM system. This process allowed them to drive adoption from the front line and take action on these insights.

It was fascinating to see how customers had different needs and preferences regarding Water Pure TVT Inc.'s customer service. For example, some accounts preferred more visits while others wanted less. These differences were based on sales data and focus groups that we conducted during our research for this project.

Introducing the new set of operational roles that would be most appropriate for the customers Water Pure TVT Inc. was targeting. After consulting with us, they increased their front-line sales team by 20%. They also created additional support positions, including one focused solely on analyzing customer needs and converted those into actionable intelligence reports, allowing them to serve clients' demands better.

When Water Pure TVT Inc. introduced its new front-line sales systems, it was clear that this would be a historic win for all parties involved. The company's representatives were thrilled to adopt these innovative tools and use data analytics to strengthen connections with customers who had been missing before they were ever even aware of its existence.

CASE STUDY 6
REMOTE CO INC. THINKS
LOCAL TO INCREASE SALES

Remote Co Inc.'s growth strategy was in danger of collapsing. We helped them to decentralize their system instead of following a standardized approach that catered strictly for national needs and increased revenue tremendously by localizing products according to with the individual demands made on each market they served.

The leading firm found themselves suffering from plummeting sales as well. However, our team came up with an innovative solution that allowed Remote Co Inc. not only to survive but thrive—all thanks to some fresh thinking about how best to handle product selection processes domestically.

REALIZED GROWTH

Staffing over an 4-month period: 40%

Revenue growth over a 5-month period: 102% increase

THE PIVOT

Remote Co Inc. not paying enough attention to local customer demographics. Instead, they had a generic approach that didn't consider where people lived or what they wanted. This ultimately limited their growth potential because there were many other factors out of their control.

To increase revenues and maximize efficiency, Remote Co Inc. took advantage of its scale by focusing on customer acquisition strategies like connecting with potential customers interested in what they sold and making their products more accessible through discounts or coupons. This allowed them to reach new consumers and generate leads that would eventually become paying clients.

Remote Co Inc. had to find a new way of doing things. They started by looking at their competitors and seeing what they were doing well—which turned out not to be much. The whole process felt stagnant, so it needed an upgrade, or they could potentially fail like many others before they did when consumers changed preferences without any warning signs.

The CEO of Remote Co Inc. knew that something had to change for their sales not only to make a comeback but exceed expectations. The pressure from competitors and investors alike were becoming too much, so he found an innovative solution: outsourcing only certain parts of the business, which helped him maintain control while still achieving desirable results at all times.

OUR APPROACH IN SEGMENTS

Customizing our services to local clients is over 100% more effective than providing them globally. With just 10–15%, we made the business stand out from competitors and increased revenue per customer. We designed a pilot project to identify localization possibilities with senior management.

The process involved four steps:

1. To identify the areas in the local market that needed more service, we performed an assortment analysis. This helped determine what services were currently being offered and where gaps might exist for potential new clients or customers interested in buying.

2. To spot growth opportunities in sales, it was vital to collaborate with their vendors.

3. Customer research was one way to understand the customers and their needs. We could learn more about them by asking questions like, "What do I need from my customer experience?" or "How does this product make you feel?"

4. Get management's input on decisions to make regarding the business.

To ensure that Remote Co Inc.'s offerings were tailored to meet customer needs, we recommended starting localization pilots across various locations and sizes. The goal was for this process was to help figure out what worked best in multiple places before rolling it out more widely across all areas where they operated.

We gathered information from managers to create a database of services tailored for different budgets. We had to make critical changes and see if it would succeed in reaching its potential growth rate and identify what was successful about our previous attempts at launching similar programs or projects like this one to repeat those successes with future endeavors.

Managers needed to have the power and freedom to make decisions. This way, they could select services that best suited their needs at a local level without being hindered by centralized policies or restrictions on what options were available within an area's budget range—giving each customer more attention than before.

There was a need to lead an organization-wide management initiative in this new localized strategy. It meant developing and implementing processes that ensured all employees were aware of their role in supporting the localized strategy goals by providing resources so they could do just that.

CASE STUDY 7
BSC SALES LTD. LEADERSHIP
REALIZED THROUGH C-SUITE
TRANSFORMATION

BSC Sales Ltd. was in a difficult position with high costs and a stretched business model. We helped them reduce expenses by over 88%, restructure their strategy for success to cut down on cost-drivers that were hurting the company financially, while still winning new clients through competitive pricing deals and personalized customer service. The turnaround has been successful: revenue is up and their financial situation has been reestablished.

REALIZED GROWTH

Staffing over a 5-month period: 15%

Revenue growth over a 8-month period: 165% increase

THE PIVOT

The crisis at BSC Sales Ltd. directly resulted from missing out on essential changes in its industry and not focusing enough on what it did best. As markets changed, so too did customer needs, which forced them to lose business opportunities because there wasn't any clear focus or direction for this firm's growth strategies moving forward.

BSC Sales Ltd. faced intense competition in the market, which led to a need for transformation. To re-establish itself as the leader of its industry groupings, the management made some crucial strategic decisions to achieve success.

They've come quietly far by using innovative ideas (e.g., discounting products with low margins or sacrificing volume at certain times) if it meant maximizing profit within an individual customer segment.

Together, we made the necessary operational changes to keep their business running smoothly and with increased efficiency. Plus, we explored strategies for future success, such as the following:

Step 1: Embracing lean techniques to cut your operational costs will help you create a more efficient business. It's also an opportunity for quick wins that can lead to financial freedom and success.

Step 2: It is crucial to launch a new set of initiatives to increase customer loyalty and retention. In addition, you need to keep up with industry standards to be successful.

Step 3: The organization might need to be restructured to be aligned with the new strategy.

The company was helped by our team where we strongly focused on cost management. We also helped them redefine their core business to build a new overall strategy with a fresh perspective.

We also redefined their brand, their outward-facing image. We focused on what they stood for, how people perceived them (reputation), and identifying strengths and gaps within their current operations vs. their desired future state.

The company used innovative ways to cut costs and reduce its real estate footprint. It also reduced the cost of advertising, which eliminated 15% from initial expenses. The business realized that streamlining certain aspects could drastically decrease how much money was being spent on employee wages or rent for offices. These savings were then reinvested into products.

BSC Sales Ltd.'s new strategy was focused on customer loyalty. As a result, they began closely tracking their existing customers to refocus the business and identify different ways to interact with them to maintain high satisfaction levels.

CASE STUDY 8
STAFFING SOLUTIONS 123
EMPLOYEES INSPIRED AS
OWNERS VIA THE CO-OP
MODEL

Staffing Solutions 123 had a problem with low customer loyalty and employee morale. This affected their revenue stream, so they implemented an incentive program that focused on performance instead of hours worked for employees and improved the quality of service provided. They increased retention rates, which led directly to better business operations, including profit margins and overall sales numbers. Improved client satisfaction also translated into increased profits even sooner than expected.

REALIZED GROWTH

Staffing over a 9-month period: 35%

Revenue growth over a 2-month period: 250% increase

THE PIVOT

Staffing Solutions 123 is a renowned US-based staffing agency, known for its customer service. However, they were experiencing a decrease in revenues and needed an influx to get them through until the next season started up.

Staffing Solutions123 was in a tough spot. The outlook for their industry and customer base was bleak, leading them to seek help from other companies that specialize in business strategy, like ours. We're happy we could be there when they needed our expertise because it seems as though things are finally looking up, and staff defections have slowed down considerably over recent months.

The goal of our project was to find out what is driving loyalty and retention in both customers and employees. We did this by identifying key factors affecting these two metrics and then designing a strategy to reduce declining revenues while increasing top employee retention rates.

We identified three primary sources.

1. The value people get from their purchases
2. How easy it was to acquire those products or services (i e., whether there's an easier way)
3. Whether you feel like your investment paid off after using something; whether they come with lasting benefits like healthier living habits

The most important thing for a company to have in their customer service strategy is understanding what makes customers tick. We talked with many current and past clients about how they make decisions on who gets helped next, and what drives them toward loyalty or away from it quicker than any other factor.

We combined this study with a larger one that examined the frontline sales managers of our client. We found that their tenure, customer satisfaction/retention rates, and profitability are all strongly correlated. The more time you spend working in these areas means greater chances for success.

The company made strategic decisions that had a significant impact on the success of its initiatives. For example, a performance-based incentive was created to increase profits and stay competitive with other companies implementing similar programs for managers. This would allow the company to control how employees perform and increase motivation through recognition and opportunities such as trips or free memberships at country clubs, depending on what type is needed.

In a short time, the new initiatives were well received and immediately impacted company culture. The pay scheme improved morale as it was more in line with what employees expect for their hard work; this led to increased sales which also helped improve training processes, among other things.

We supported these efforts by improving the business's existing solutions while adding value through innovative thinking—all without disrupting any ongoing projects or commitments.

The innovative solutions of our team enabled us to create a single strategy that could be applied across the entire client's business.

CASE STUDY 9
LG ENTERPRISES LLC. MICRO-PIVOTS POWERED A BRAND AND SKYROCKETED SALES

With the help of our Micro-Pivot System, Global Insurance Lead Gen Provider was able to relaunch their brand and increase sales with premium lead generation. Achieving this success required a shift for three strategies that were pilot-tested with excellent results:

1. Digital footprint improvement through increased social media followers and influencers

2. Advertising on other platforms like Instagram where they would not have been generally advertised before

3. Buying experience enhancements including better protection against fraudulent transactions as well as ease customer service when dealing directly with clients online

REALIZED GROWTH

Staffing over a 4-month period: 25%

Revenue growth over a 6-month period: 125% increase

THE PIVOT

We came up with a plan to help LG Enterprises LLC grow quickly. It was clear that they needed more than just our services; they also had some old-fashioned cleaning needs. We this organization to see the diverse range of professionals working together on projects that would revitalize their brand and boost business growth rates across departments. But not before making sure all employees felt included in what's happening inside each other's heads (and out).

The Micro-Pivot System is an excellent strategy for attacking goals that are quickly validated with customers. The system can be scaled across the organization once it has been proven successful in one area, making this approach preferable if you're looking to make quick changes and have flexible options at hand when tackling new challenges

LG Enterprises LLC created three micro-pivots.

- An innovative approach to customer service can be a hit with customers, and it could even help your company grow. Professionalism is vital when you want people's loyalty- don't just provide them something they need or want; give them an experience that makes the journey worthwhile for both sides of things.

- We can use AI and machine learning to improve the company's digital touchpoints. These tools will make it easier for a business owner or manager who strives for customer service excellence. In addition, they'll help eliminate some time-consuming tasks by handling the process themselves.

- Social media is a powerful way to increase brand awareness, engagement, and advocacy. It can also help you find customer testimonials for your business and generate leads from social networks.

LG Enterprises LLC is a company that has been known for using A/B testing, customer feedback, and agile innovation. They have developed specific action plans for each micro-pivot they've experienced to maintain their competitive edge over other companies.

Enhanced customer experience increased referrals via social media. All these factors combined helped increase sales through the company's digital platforms.

The Micro-Pivot System from LG Enterprises LLC has been proven time after again as a successful technique for managing your business on all channels, including Facebook ads. It targets specific demographics that keep followers engaged with timely content while building trust among them at an increasing rate each day.

Customers are much more likely to purchase from a trained professional, primarily due to the company's recent redesigns. The new leads attending micro-pivots have been near twice as reliable as their peers who deal directly (78%). With an 86% rating, these transactions are highly refined. Not only do we see an increase of customers visiting your site but also sign-ups coming soon on track for thousands per year by 2022.

CASE STUDY 10
PM ESSENTIAL INC. VISION THAT TRANSFORMED THE COMPANY TO NEW HEIGHTS

PM Essential Inc. was not performing well due to a lack of organizational structure and vision. There was very little coordination between staff members, which led them not to be aligned with any new goals or ideas for their company. Our team focused on helping this business achieve through leadership development programs and strategic decision-making methods like incentives so they could hit those milestones more efficiently.

REALIZED GROWTH

Staffing over a 12-month period: 0%

Revenue growth over a 8-month period: 300% increase

THE PIVOT

PM Essential Inc. is a global company with an established history of success. However, it had been losing market share to another larger competitor for some time. It needed to keep up by making changes to move forward effectively into the next decade.

The company's strategy was built around a local marketplace. There were no centralized mechanisms for coordination or decision-making, which led to inefficiencies across the board as each team searched out its solutions without any input from others on what needed doing first. Effects ranged 100% toward focusing solely on their areas of responsibility rather than considering how it affected other departments/functions outside one's duties.

A lack of central planning functions left everything with untrained leaders who found themselves making decisions quickly under pressure with little guidance available beyond whatever information they could gather.

The CEO of PM Essential Inc., a global brand with the goal to leverage scale more effectively and retain decentralized decision-making, is driven by his passion for building successful businesses.

A three-phased organizational transformation was our approach. In the first phase, we set up a strong foundation for change by getting all key stakeholders on board and clarifying their visions of success with this new system. In addition, they learned how it would work operationally through tests run internally and externally among customers/stakeholders before implementation began.

Next, so that everyone had enough time, they were prepared emotionally and cognitively to know what information needed to be delivered without any surprises. And last, which helped make these transitions much smoother, the entire organization was aligned with a new vision, which helped the company progress significantly.

Leadership: We were able to take our client's vision for global brand and convert it into clear goals, aligning organizational systems around these goals.

Decision-making: We assisted PM Essential Inc. in successfully defining roles, assigning responsibilities, and making decisions that would impact international markets.

Incentives and measures: We recommended that PM Essential Inc. reorient its metrics toward a milestone-based business. This will help them focus more on short-term gains and long-term success, which companies like this need.

CASE STUDY 11
SMQT CONSTRUCTION HAS AN UNUSUAL SPIN AND SALES COMP PLAN THAT USES A UNIQUE METRIC

SMQT Construction realized it needed to change a few things to maintain its revenue. One of these critical changes included increasing discount rates on vendors and rebates, which increased opportunities and success in the business.

REALIZED GROWTH

Staffing over a 2-month period: 10%

Revenue growth over a 12-month period: 400% increase

THE PIVOT

How do you make the most of a construction company with ten different divisions? Take one look at SMQT Construction, and their situation was clear. Divisions had separate sales organizations, incentive structures, and profitability goals. Unfortunately, it was not working for them anymore, so we helped to create an integrated compensation package in just five weeks that aligned perfectly to both corporate objectives and kept overall commission costs consistent across all units.

We know what it takes when there's no time or money: focused strategy paired up against daunting tasks, along with strong communication skills ensuring everyone shares input equally.

We first compiled data on their compensation levels and structures to create an indepth evaluation of SMQT Construction's sales force. Next, data was collected through interviews and analysis involving company records such as profit contribution reports from each division, along with information about enabling technology that could be used by any business unit ready for change or not considering a technological upgrade.

The company's strategy was to focus on core competencies and not get distracted by short-term incentives. Unfortunately, this caused a problem with how salespeople were being supported. It became especially difficult when different divisions had different goals after discounts or rebates. Some only wanted more profits, while others only cared about market share based on their own identity within the industry.

The result? Sales representatives felt left out since they couldn't measure profitability relating to any changes made from one period compared to another. There wasn't an overall picture, so they didn't always know if their efforts were successful.

To understand the granular effect and predict changes in compensation for highly productive employees, we modeled

SMQT Construction's financials individually. This allowed us to see how different models could impact specific people with varying productivity levels.

A 2011 study found that when human resource professionals consider factors such as age or education level and job responsibilities, there is significant variation among workers' earnings. Considering these differences before calculating annual salaries allowed them to make fair adjustments and retain top talent through increased wages.

In a move that should increase profitability, we recommended SMQT Construction's new rate structure and compensation plan. The short-term inclusion of gross margin metrics was also included to encourage vendors to shift toward more profitable ones by tiering them on after discounts or rebates have been taken into account. This change fit with their objectives perfectly.

We knew that this would be a considerable undertaking, so we first prepared by mapping the process and assessing risks before identifying critical stakeholders for their input on how best to tackle such an ambitious task. Next came launching an aggressive marketing strategy to generate revenue from all those interested enough (and able) to buy into what they were offering.

CASE STUDY 12
MED STOP INC. SERVICES
CREATED THE IDEAL
COMPETITIVE ADVANTAGE

Med Stop Inc. was a company with intense margin pressure, so they sought ways to grow their business. We were able to develop an innovative new strategy that would meet those needs; the result being our completely redesigned service program.

REALIZED GROWTH

Staffing over a 12-month period: 0%

Revenue growth over a 4-month period: 123% increase

THE PIVOT

Med Stop Inc. needed to create a clear plan to allow them access to their full potential and devise an actionable "how-to win" strategy for their business venture. For example, this company specializes in medical equipment supply needs for hospitals or clinics with modern technology requirements like surgical instruments without compromising patient safety.

Med Stop Inc.'s marketing and business development team worked to harmonize the company's service-product portfolio while also developing a systematic approach towards M&A. The goal was for them to expand their capabilities by filling gaps to meet customer needs as well as adding new ones along the way

Understanding the needs and wants of your customers is a crucial element in creating products that will satisfy them. This includes understanding their financial capabilities and what drives customer value, from pricing to features to support options. By analyzing all aspects of selling goods or services, you can ensure everything falls into place so customers continue coming back time after time without hesitation. This ultimately drives up revenue over long periods because every sale matters more when there's less competition out on the streets. Plus, increased loyalty means happier consumers.

There are ways to create a system that fosters organizational learning. The first way is by focusing on the needs and wants of the customer. This leads to feedback from those who have already purchased something from the business. This helps shape future operations as well. In addition, observations were made through strategic monitoring tools.

Every company needs to incorporate customer service into its research and development processes. R&D services should be designed to offer customers earth-shaking services, but only if those initiatives meet both business goals and technical requirements for innovation success.

People are the heart of any company, and culture keeps them happy. This includes processes to recruit new employees and train those hired so everyone's strengths can be used efficiently and addressing safety concerns when they arise so no one feels left out or ignored.

With efficient supply chain processes, operations ensure that the right parts are available and quickly delivered.

We helped Med Stop Inc. transform from a small business that received little attention to an economic engine for growth. Today, their service culture extends beyond the company's walls and into every corner of its ecosystem, inspiring customers and employees alike with one goal: sustainable success.

CASE STUDY 13
TECH P&Q POWERS AI TO
INCREASE CROSS-SELLING

Tech P&Q increased its data analytics investments to support a more strategic, focused approach. In addition, they renovated technology and human resources to showcase the results of these efforts with even greater speediness than before.

REALIZED GROWTH

Staffing over a 7-month period: 22%

Revenue growth over a 7-month period: 109% increase

THE PIVOT

Tech P&Q wanted to achieve its analytics goals. They became our partner in a five-part plan.

The team found a high-value opportunity and realized that their innovative approach could yield meaningful results. The group consisted of a sponsor and operational people who provided full-time coding skills for an analytics system. They were also responsible for recruiting other people. The operational person's responsibility was overseeing daily operations to keep things running smoothly during development cycles. The team's goal was to make sure all went well by managing various marketing strategy aspects and focusing on cross-selling potential.

We assessed Tech P&Q's current portfolio and cross-selling performance with careful analysis. We created customer profiles to explore personal events that triggered additional product sales and contract details. They had over ten years' worth of data to make better business decisions about where their focus should be on future investments or marketing efforts as we advanced.

A data lake is the lifeblood of any company, containing information on everything from customer preferences to product catalogs. This one had more than 20 databases storing insights about shoppers and their habits over the past ten years, including client-side code that helps predict what they'll buy along with external sources like social media channels where customers share feedback.

Our success was mainly due to the agile development methods used. The team was able to break down the project into separate sprints that covered every core task from data prep and loading, all while staying close enough to avoid missing any important information or knowledge transfer opportunities between developers working on the different parts.

The project also included challenging the established beliefs of top management. Weekly meetings ensured any roadblocks would be addressed quickly and effectively so that all levers affecting cross-selling could also come into play. Maintaining an open dialogue with the team was crucial for customer engagement initiatives.

In addition, we recommended structured documentation and version control, which helped tackle some complex coding tasks previously beyond reach. The team's work was crucial for helping the client improve their skills. In addition, the team provided structured documentation and version control, which helped tackle some complex coding tasks previously beyond reach for this project.

CASE STUDY 14
BD, LLC. DISCOVERS HOW
MUCH BRANDING MATTERS

BD, LLC. was losing market share due to stiff competition in its formerly profitable service lines. We reviewed their product portfolio and suggested that it reposition itself to offer high-end, more profitable service offerings. Our client saw a significant increase in net present value and reversed its decline in market share.

REALIZED GROWTH

Staffing over a 8-month period: 35%

Revenue growth over a 5-month period: 255% increase

THE PIVOT

To analyze each product, we used an analytical approach that was both high-road and low-road. The process allowed us to determine the best course of action for the business by aligning it with the quadrant within this framework. We know how vital customer insights are when making strategic decisions about the company's future.

We helped the company reposition itself as an industry leader by focusing on its high-end service offerings with higher margins. The required additional advertising resources and rebuilding of assets were necessary for this strategy to work effectively.

Those included:

A website overhaul. A new website can make a business look more professional, modern, and appealing. The right design will help the business reach potential customers efficiently while also providing them with the information they need to learn about what they offer and how they might get in contact.

All platforms got a social media overhaul. To give every platform the best chance of success, all social media channels received a significant a makeover.

Systems were redesigned from front to back. It was time to redesign the back end of the business. In today's world, we no longer see systems improved or redesigned on an isolated basis; they are integrated for better efficiency.

Tools for process management. Process management tools can be a great way to streamline workflow more efficiently. Many programs offer process automation, allowing the business to assign tasks or send invoices without an in-house employee for each function

A 12-month marketing strategy that is flexible and adaptable We helped the company establish a 12-month marketing strategy that was flexible and adaptable. With the latest social media tools, we equiped the team with designs for today's digital world so they're not left behind in this fast-paced era of instant and ultra-communication.

Rebrand complete to position in the market. The first step was to assess whether or not everything about the branding matched what the customers were looking for these days. This meant taking the time to doing significant research before jumping headfirst into any rebranding efforts.

With the long-term growth of the company in mind, we implemented an important documentation overhaul. After implementing our recommended strategies, BD, LLC has seen market share declines reversed.

CASE STUDY 15
TCM PLUMBING, LLC. CREATED SAVINGS BY OUTSOURCING PROCUREMENT IN A UNSTABLE ENVIRONMENT

When TCM Plumbing LLC. reduced costs, they found that it was insufficient to boost their profits. They needed additional savings to continue doing well and keep growing like before. We were able to identify strategies to help our them reduce expenses without sacrificing service quality or employee satisfaction because we're all about balance. Our reorganization of procurement processes saved them money while also providing better customer care throughout this whole process. As a result, there have been rapid gains with long-term performance achieved faster than anyone imagined possible.

REALIZED GROWTH

Staffing over a 12-month period: 10%

Revenue growth over a 6-month period: 154% increase

THE PIVOT

Our goal was to identify all savings opportunities and critical enablers to sustainable results through our extensive diagnostic work. The process includes looking at the organization as a whole and tier levels of management, identifying what was working so they could build upon that success moving forward.

The diagnostic identified 350 cost-saving strategies and critical stakeholders. It found all the savings opportunities that could be used to save 11%. This included standardizing more components, increasing reliance upon low-cost sourcing, and a variety of other factors like optimizing workflow processes or tightening up supply chains. It's essential for companies with growing businesses because they're always looking at ways to lower expenses without harming their bottom line too much.

To maximize the organization's impact, it's necessary to implement initiatives in waves. Each category should have its own set of targeted and prioritized projects aligned with one another so you can save money on unnecessary costs while still seeing success.

Empowering purchasing professionals and enabling them to make more informed decisions helps save time. Our services range from enhancing capabilities for strategic sourcing in the region of their choice up to training on negotiation techniques.

A good project management tool allows better visibility into the company's needs and requirements as they arise on an ongoing basis, so there are no surprises or setbacks downline.

We were also working hard behind the scenes at making purchasing processes more efficient by implementing changes in how products get sourced. This means less time spent looking through lists waiting until something comes along just right; instead, everything should be available within minutes.

Senior management will act on our recommendations to reduce purchasing costs. These steps will help limit the financial drain of unnecessary spending and ensure sustainable growth in future years.

Negotiation prep is an essential part of any successful business deal. To gain a competitive edge with suppliers, arm negotiators in cost analysis and pricing information, as well as role-play negotiations before tough talks are underway.

It is essential to have a comprehensive sourcing strategy to find the most cost-effective suppliers. Therefore, regional markets with significant structural advantages will be more fruitful than smaller regions and countries lacking these factors in their economic system. A good way of finding high-quality products at reasonable prices can involve working closely together as a partnership between the company or business organization's needs versus what they offer available through local vendors who live within proximity where you operate.

The best way to avoid being dependent on just one supplier is by clearly defining your specifications for requests-for-proposal (RFPs). You can also consider other sourcing options if you're looking at broader market conditions or want something specific that isn't available through an established vendor pipeline.

Improve testing efficiency by facilitating supplier approval. The process for accepting or denying a new supplier should be clear, consistent, and executed quickly so that your organization can remain focused on its goals while still meeting demand from suppliers who want to sell products within the company's standards.

Accountability and transparency are of great importance. Results should be reported regularly to ensure that the initiative is successful and countermeasures, if necessary, for improvement or change in strategy.

Output. An excellent way to implement savings programs successfully would involve careful planning and monitoring the progress to see what's working well before taking any further steps forward.

TCM Plumbing LLC.'s senior management team established a clear sourcing strategy and action plan to achieve the aggressive savings targets for the fiscal year. This allowed them to reposition themselves within their industry by aligning all aspects of operations with client needs, including product quality standards raised higher than ever before to maintain the business growth trajectory.

THE STRATEGIC ADVISOR BOARD

The Strategic Advisor Board is a dynamic team that partners with your business to create custom strategies to help you grow your business on multiple levels. We look at the core foundation and systems within your current business to refine approaches, establish cost-saving measures, and ensure your systems are functioning at the highest efficiency and profitability. We add value to your business to place your business in the best position to implement strategies to scale.

We help businesses emerge from the growth to scale. When a small business grows, resources are added, employees are hired to serve more clients, and strength is added to the business within operations. Scaling your business is where you reframe your brand, automate many of your practices, and create strategic partnerships to begin the process to expand your influence in the marketplace. A comprehensive strategy, a team to support your business, and a trusted network of business service providers is what the Strategic Advisor Board offers to help your business grow into an influential brand.

Our multifaceted and dynamic approach to partnering to develop custom strategies to grow and scale your business is unique in the marketplace.

Are you ready to take the next step in your business?

Learn more at www.strategicadvisorboard.com.